What Reader

Life Lessons fro

Finding God in America's Most Glorious Places

This book fascinated me. Despite the obvious title, Musco's book doesn't fall into a neat category. Many may easily overlook the delightful, easy-to-read book. Musco gives the background to the various national parks, including interesting trivia, and spotlights one particular historical aspect. From that focus, she moves into a spiritual life lesson.

—**Cecil Murphey,** author or co-author of more than 130 books, including *Gifted Hands: The Ben Carson Story* and *90 Minutes in Heaven* with Don Piper

* * *

I very much enjoyed reading this book about more than forty of the national parks, monuments, historical parks, national memorials, military parks, and other national shrines run by the National Park Service. I especially liked all the interesting historical tidbits. I found the spiritual applications and life lessons uplifting. I wholeheartedly endorse this book.

—**Michael J. Oard,** co-author of "True North National Park Series," including *Your Guide to Zion and Bryce Canyon National Parks, Your Guide to the Grand Canyon,* and *Your Guide to Yellowstone and Grand Teton National Parks*

* * *

As a Christian, a hiker, and a lover of parks and wooded areas, I'm impressed with Penny Musco's effort to combine powerful devotional thoughts and challenges with highly descriptive narratives of many of our country's finest National Parks and Monuments. The extra information about tours, accommodations, and amenities are a nice bonus! This will become an often- consulted reference book in our home.

—**Mike Owen,** devotional writer, published in *Blessings from the Blue Ridge*

* * *

I love the workable tips and unique insights presented by Penny Musco. This book, spiced with humor and encouragement, propels me to a greater appreciation of our national parks...and a deeper relationship with the Creator.

—**Linda Turner**, award-winning poet, inspirational speaker, and aspiring novelist

* * *

Life Lessons is an enjoyable read. The author deftly relates insights from the beauty of God's creation to meaningful life lessons from his Word. The nuggets of American history interspersed throughout the book provide some interesting factoids that aren't necessarily included in the formal education everyone receives. We especially loved learning about the lesser-known parks.

—**Rick Triplett**, Bible teacher, author of *Living by Faith in an Unfaithful World*
—**Donna Triplett**, editor and multi-published devotional and short story writer with work appearing in *Blessings from the Blue Ridge* and *Penned from the Heart*

Life Lessons
FROM THE NATIONAL PARKS

Meeting God in America's
Most Glorious Places

PENNY MUSCO

SONFIRE MEDIA
A PUBLISHING COMPANY
GALAX, VIRGINIA

*Life Lessons from the National Parks: Finding God in
America's Most Glorious Places*

Published by Sonfire Media, LLC
120 West Grayson Street, Suite 350
Galax, VA 24333 USA

Scripture is from THE HOLY BIBLE, NEW INTERNATIONAL
VERSION®, NIV® Copyright © 1973, 1978, 1984, 2011 by Biblica,
Inc.® Used by permission. All rights reserved worldwide.

Cover and interior book design by Larry W. Van Hoose

ISBN No. 978-0-9891064-6-7

To Mom, who always supports my dreams;

to Joe, who helps make them happen;

and to Mimi, a dream come true.

Table of Contents

🍁 FALL

❄️ WINTER

Acknowledgments

Here's where I get to express my deep appreciation to my editor, Vie Herlocker, for holding my hand—over the phone and by email—praying for me, and sending candy. Vie, your editing has made me a better writer, and I'm very grateful. Thanks also to the entire team at Sonfire Media for believing in this book and bringing it to fruition.

To those who gave their endorsements to *Life Lessons from the National Parks*, a huge thanks. Your support means so much.

I'm also appreciative of the people who took time to read my manuscript to correct mistakes and offer advice—Mike, Linda, Rick, Donna, and Carol. Any other errors are on me.

A big thank you to friends and family who asked how the book was coming along as I sweated through the process. Sitting alone in front of a computer screen wrestling with words and concepts usually is a fun challenge, but sometimes it's just grueling. Your thoughtfulness made the job less lonely.

Finally, to my terrific husband, who listens patiently, calms me when I'm stressed, and believes in me even when I don't: I hope I tell you enough how much you mean to me. I really, really couldn't have done this without you.

Writing in Capitals

For since the creation of the world, God's invisible qualities—his eternal power and divine nature—have been clearly seen, being understood from what has been made, so that people are without excuse. Romans 1:20

The above verse observes that God's characteristics reveal themselves in the world he formed. Our national parks may be our country's "best idea," as historian, environmentalist, and author Wallace Stegner said, but they were God's idea first!

There are many books about the parks, but few approach them from a Christian perspective. That's a shame, considering that John Muir, whom many call the Father of the National Park Service, unequivocally and unapologetically linked the splendor he saw around him with its Designer:

> I am sitting here in a little shanty made of sugar pine shingles this Sabbath evening. I have not been at church a single time since leaving home. Yet this glorious valley [Yosemite] might well be called a church, for every lover of the great Creator who comes within the broad overwhelming influences of the place fails not to worship as he never did before. The glory of the Lord is upon all his works; it is written plainly upon all the fields of every clime, and upon every sky, but here in this place of surpassing glory the Lord has written in capitals.(Badé 1924, 209)

My family and I have visited many national parks over the years. As we hiked, paddled, and biked through them, we recognized and appreciated God's handiwork. But I didn't realize, until a trip to the

Florida Everglades, how many of God's specific attributes I found reflected among the park's natural elements and stories. The more I looked, the more I found.

"I'm going to start a blog, and call it *Life Lessons from the National Parks*," I told my husband on that winter day in 2009. "Will you set it up for me?"

Wonderful guy that he is, he did. I began sharing my observations online, and eventually those meditations came together in the book you now hold in your hand.

I've divided the book into four sections, corresponding to the seasons, into which the parks' cycles of history, anniversaries, and activities naturally fit. Lessons are found in each one; we only have to open our eyes to what God wants to teach us.

I hope you enjoy the journey as much as I have. I pray you'll see not my words in these pages, but the Lord's, who really does express himself in capital letters.

Spring

(handwritten notes at top of page) Must put up w/ painful pruning on earth to have beautiful buds. Life is short + precious: similar to that of a cherry blossom.

Spring Is Sprung!
National Mall & Memorial Parks

See! The winter is past; the rains are over and gone. Flowers appear on the earth; the season of singing has come, the cooing of doves is heard in our land. The fig tree forms its early fruit; the blossoming vines spread their fragrance.

Song of Songs 2:11-13

Is any season more welcome than spring? A taste of warmth, early flowers poking their way out of the ground ... such a delight after a cold and snowy winter!

For me, cherry blossoms are one of the greatest harbingers of spring, and our nation's capital has masses of them planted around the Tidal Basin and Potomac River. They're a lovely feature of the more than one thousand acres that make up the National Mall & Memorial Parks, part of the National Park Service. "America's Front Yard" stretches from the Capitol building to the Potomac and is scattered with some of our most iconic monuments and memorials, commemorating wars and people.

The annual Cherry Blossom Festival is a glorious event held every spring in Washington, D. C. Festival dates change every year, depending upon the temperatures, but usually peak bloom time is late March or early April. Festival activities, though, go on through April.

Getting cherry trees planted in the District of Columbia wasn't an easy task. Mrs. Eliza Ruhamah Scidmore first put forth the idea after a visit to Japan in 1885. Soon other advocates joined her quest. Scidmore decided to raise money for the project herself, and contacted First Lady Helen Taft for assistance. In August 1909 the Japanese Embassy pledged to donate two thousand cherry trees, which arrived the following January.

Unfortunately the trees were diseased and had to be burned. It wasn't until March 1912 that 3,020 bug-free cherry trees of twelve varieties arrived. Mrs. Taft and Viscountess Iwa Chinda, wife of the Japanese ambassador, ceremonially planted two of them on the Tidal Basin's northern bank, where they still stand today, several hundred yards west of the John Paul Jones Memorial, near 17th St. S.W., and marked with a plaque. Workmen planted the remainder of the trees.

In 1965 the Japanese government gave the United States an additional thirty-eight hundred trees, which were American-grown. Lady Bird Johnson and Mrs. Ryuji Takeuchi, the Japanese ambassador's wife, reenacted the initial planting ceremony. In the intervening years, the Park Service added more trees, many of them propagated from the 1912 gift.

In Japanese culture, cherry blossoms symbolize the beauty and brevity of our existence. These delicate, exquisite flowers don't last long. One minute they're buds, the next they've popped open in an array of gorgeous pink and white flowers, then suddenly the petals are littering the ground like snow.

Isn't that just like life? As kids, time seems to move so slowly, but as we age, it appears to speed up. We ask ourselves, *where did the years go?* Moses pondered this anomaly as well. "The length of our days is seventy years—or eighty, if we have the strength," he wrote in Psalm 90:10, "yet their span is but trouble and sorrow, for they quickly pass, and we fly away."

To get to the beautiful blossoming called eternal life, like the trees, we must put up with annoying infestations and painful pruning here on earth. We can't have the former without the latter. "There is a time for everything, and a season for every activity under heaven," Solomon wrote in Ecclesiastes 3:1.

But we have a Master Gardener who tends us lovingly, offering us fullness of joy and abundant life. Through every season, we hear his voice calling us to delight in his company, not just for a little while, but every day of the year and into time without end.

Thanks to him, with one eye on life's transience, we truly can bloom where we're planted.

See for Yourself

National Mall & Memorial Parks: *www.nps.gov/nama*

Washington's Metro can get you here, but plan on exploring on foot or by bicycle. In March, the Park Service issues frequent updates on the cherry trees' estimated bloom time, so the thousands of visitors can arrive at its peak. Paddleboats offer another way to view the show; visitors can rent them at the Tidal Basin Welcome Area.

The park also has an unexpected bonus—a public aquatic center and three golf courses. If you want to tour the White House, which is also part of the park, you must make a reservation in advance through your congressional representative or senator's office.

*Inspire the
hopeless with
courage
• Don't despair... God has
brought you to this
point for a reason*

In God's Place
Dry Tortugas National Park
Ford's Theatre

> *But Joseph said to them, "Don't be afraid. Am I in the place of God? You intended to harm me, but God intended it for good to accomplish what is now being done."*
>
> Genesis 50:19-20

You may recall that April 14, 1865, marks the anniversary of President Lincoln's assassination at the hands of John Wilkes Booth, at Ford's Theatre in Washington, D.C. What you might be surprised to learn is that this theatre is part of the National Park Service. While the playhouse is a fascinating place to visit, it was at another Park Service location where I first heard a riveting story connected with this history-altering act.

Booth broke a leg in his haste to escape after shooting the president. Fleeing on horseback through the Maryland countryside the following day, he stopped at the farm of an acquaintance, Dr. Samuel Mudd, who set the damaged limb.

Eight people were tried and found guilty of conspiring or aiding in the murder, including Dr. Mudd (Booth had been killed in the manhunt). Four of them were hanged. Mudd and the others were sent to the military jail at Fort Jefferson, now part of Dry Tortugas National Park, located about seventy miles west of Key West in the Gulf of Mexico.

My husband and I vacationed in southern Florida's trio of national parks during one memorable trip. After enjoying Everglades and Biscayne, we drove three hours down to Key West, the continental United States' southernmost city, and the next day boarded a boat to head to Dry Tortugas.

Garden Key, where the fort is situated, is part of a chain of small islands, or keys, which make up the park. Our boat supplied everything we needed for a fun, carefree day—snorkeling equipment, unlimited food and beverages, and restrooms.

We had it so much better than Dr. Mudd and his fellow inmates. Dry Tortugas came by its name because turtles (*tortugas*, in Spanish) are plentiful—but fresh water is not. In summer, temperatures soar and mosquitoes swarm. Life at Fort Jefferson in the mid-1800s meant desolation, heat, bugs, hard labor, and rationed water.

During Dr. Mudd's incarceration, a yellow fever epidemic broke out. The staff physician died, so Dr. Mudd took over his duties. In gratitude, three hundred soldiers petitioned President Andrew Johnson to grant Dr. Mudd pardon, writing, "He inspired the hopeless with courage, and by his constant presence in the midst of danger and infection, regardless of his own life, tranquilized the fearful and desponding" (Summers, 2009, 1).

President Johnson granted the request. Dr. Mudd left the prison in March of 1869, and lived his final years as a free man.

During a tour of Fort Jefferson, as I listened to a park ranger relate Dr. Mudd's story, I thought of Joseph in the Old Testament book of Genesis. He too went through bad times and good. His jealous brothers sold him as a slave, but God provided a good job for him. Then he was jailed because of false accusations. After a long stint in prison, Joseph got out and became second in command in Egypt. The same brothers who betrayed him ended up coming to him for help during a famine. Joseph not only provided for them, but also forgave them when they feared retribution.

Perhaps you too have found yourself in difficult circumstances like Dr. Mudd and Joseph. Maybe you realize you could have done something differently, but the consequences were too severe. Scripture implies that Joseph lorded his status as favorite son over his brothers, but their payback went way beyond the offense. Or maybe you're like Dr. Mudd, in misery because of a stupid mistake (historians believe he probably wasn't part of the original plot, but was guilty of not alerting authorities to Booth's whereabouts), and now you're paying dearly, with plenty of time for regret.

small "mistakes", but overwhelming consequence

Or you could be in trouble through no fault of your own. On her very first day of her senior year of high school, proudly driving her new-to-her car, my daughter Mimi was T-boned by a careless driver. No one was hurt, thankfully, but the damage totaled nearly $6,000. The kicker was that *she* got a ticket and four points on her license. It took a lawyer, three court appearances, and several months before the truth emerged, the court dropped the charges, and her car was repaired.

Three years later, the car was finished off when a teenager on her cell phone ran a red light. Mimi and her passenger received only minor injuries—thank God for air bags! But then her passenger's mother sued Mimi, even though witnesses and both insurance companies agreed she wasn't to blame. After a year, the court dismissed the claim, but we all experienced a lot of anger, bewilderment, and frustration because of the incident.

Joseph's words are a message for all who suffer: Don't give in to despair! God has brought you to this point for a reason.

I don't presume to know what he's doing in your life—and I sure can't always figure out what he's up to in mine—but you and I can be certain that the same One who guided Joseph through his triumphs and trials will see us through as well. In whatever dry and deserted place we find ourselves, God is accomplishing something in and through us that couldn't have happened otherwise. We may not understand it, and we certainly don't enjoy the process, but when we hold on and trust him, we can battle through the fear, hurt, and anguish, and emerge victorious.

Like Dr. Mudd, may each of us—because of or in spite of our tough times—display courage and extend hope to others. Like Joseph, may we forgive those who harm us, and take heart because we rest securely in God's place.

[handwritten margin note: We don't always understand the trials but we can take hope that God is changing us through them + we can be victorious.]

See for Yourself

Dry Tortugas National Park: *www.nps.gov/drto*

Fort Jefferson is a crumbling, six-sided, never-completed garrison with two thousand archways, spiral staircases made entirely of granite, and an elaborate system of sand-filtered cisterns to capture rainwater. The park is a bird watcher's dream: three hundred thousand birds pass through the Tortugas annually. And the clear, shallow waters surrounding the fort reveal a myriad of God's lavish designs, including lavender sea fans, brown sponges, red coral, and brightly colored fish. Scuba enthusiasts can even scope out a few shipwrecks.

Ford's Theatre: *www.nps.gov/foth*

Timed tickets are required for entry to this working theatre, as well as the museum and Peterson House, and it's best to reserve one online. Same day tickets may not be available. The mortally wounded president was carried to the Peterson House that fateful night, where he died the next morning. The adjacent Center for Education and Leadership explores the immediate aftermath of Lincoln's death and his continuing legacy.

God Still Speaks
Thomas Edison National Historical Park

In the past God spoke to our forefathers through the prophets at many times and in various ways, but in these last days he has spoken to us by his Son.

Hebrews 1:1-2

The Thomas Edison National Historical Park is a small gem located in West Orange, New Jersey, about fifteen miles west of Manhattan. The famed inventor's home first came under Park Service jurisdiction in 1955, his nearby laboratory the following year. The two areas combined to become the Edison National Historic Site in 1962, which then achieved its final designation as a historical park in March 2009.

Edison developed the phonograph in the 1870s. At first he used paper wrapped around a cylinder to record sounds; later he tried tin foil and then finally wax. The cylinders had many problems, though: they were fragile, only recorded two to four minutes of material, and couldn't easily be mass-produced. They were used until the late 1920s when superior disc recordings gained popularity.

In the historical site's early days, officials discovered a wooden box with two names scratched on the outside: "Edison" and

"Wangemann." Inside were brown wax recording cylinders. Through the years, officials speculated about what might be on these unlabeled recordings.

When a man named Jerry Fabris became curator of the sound recording collection at the Edison museum in 1994, he began the long process of cataloging all thirty-nine thousand wax and disc recordings in the inventory. He finally got around to the intriguing wooden box in 2005, but didn't have the equipment needed to convert the sounds from the cylinders into digital files. In 2010 the Friends of the Thomas Edison National Historical Park financed the equipment and consultant services required to do so.

When Fabris heard German, he had his first clue that he might be listening to something spectacular.

In 1889 Thomas Edison sent Theo Wangemann to display Edison Phonograph Works machines at the Paris World's Fair. While there Wangemann recorded, among other things, Johannes Brahms playing the piano (unfortunately, that cylinder was worn out before it could be copied). Then Wangemann went on to his native Germany. The recordings from that trip had been thought lost. Until Fabris uncovered them.

It took two more years and additional experts to identify the voices on the cylinder as German Chancellor Otto von Bismarck, and Helmuth von Moltke, the aide-de-camp to Kaiser Wilhelm and later chief of staff for the Prussian Army.

Moltke read Shakespeare and other literature, while Bismarck recited songs and implored his son to live morally and moderately. What they said wasn't as electrifying as the fact that the recording of Bismarck is the only one of a person born in the eighteenth century.

"In the 18th century, the human voice was described as one of the most noble capacities of human beings," wrote Stephan Puille, the German researcher who identified Bismarck's voice, in an email quoted in an Associated Press article. "Bismarck is no longer mute. I think his voice allows a new access to him." You can listen to the recording and read the transcript on the park's website.

It's easy to understand why researchers were excited to make this discovery—how amazing to be able to hear famous voices from so long ago! But you know what's even more wonderful? We have the voice of God—who's existed from eternity past—every day! We have it in the Bible—the word of God, written through the inspiration of the Holy Spirit for all to read. "For this commandment which I command you today is not too difficult for you, nor is it out of reach...But the word is very near you, in your mouth and in your heart, that you may observe it" (Deuteronomy 30:8, 10-14).

And while Moltke and Bismarck didn't say anything earth shattering, God does. He displays his power, glory, and yes, fury, through his thundering voice; yet he shows his comfort, strength, and gentleness through a whisper. Jesus spoke with equal authority, proclaiming truth, healing with just a word, and commanding the wind and rain to cease. The Holy Spirit continues his ministry of communication today.

Do you hear that voice speaking to you? I guarantee you it is the Spirit. Oh, he won't necessarily speak audibly, but you'll know when the Good Shepherd's calling because he'll make it plain. What he says will reach down into the deepest depths of your soul. And in the future will come a day "when the dead will hear the voice of the Son of God and those who hear will live" (John 5:25).

Of course, you can stop up your ears and refuse to hear or believe. The children of Israel challenged what God said and rebelled, and as a result, they were not allowed to enter the land he had promised them, but died in the wilderness. A much more dire fate awaits those who ignore God's insistent, compelling call—eternal separation from him. "See to it that you do not refuse him who speaks," the writer of Hebrews solemnly concludes. "If they did not escape when they refused him who warned them on earth, how much less will we, if we turn away from him who warns us from heaven?" (Hebrews 12:25).

As the German researcher noted, those long-ago historical voices are no longer mute, and are now accessible.

But God has never been silent.

All we have to do is listen.

See for Yourself

Thomas Edison National Historical Park: *www.nps.gov/edis*

Take a self-guided tour of Edison's laboratory, located on West Orange's Main Street, where the famed inventor, holder of 1,093 patents, improved the phonograph and built the first motion picture studio. Then, pick up a pass to see his lovely twenty-nine-room mansion nearby.

Living Water
Hot Springs National Park

Everyone who drinks this water will be thirsty again, but whoever drinks the water I give him will never thirst. Indeed, the water I give him will become in him a spring of water welling up to eternal life.

John 4:13-14

Beginning in middle school, my daughter, Mimi, set a goal to visit all fifty states. We traveled to many of them during family vacations, but as she headed off to college, she was still missing a few.

During spring break of her senior year, she and I traveled to Arkansas to check off another state on her list. We snagged a great airfare to Little Rock, explored that city for a couple of days, then drove to Hot Springs National Park, about an hour southwest of the capital city.

A little known, yet important, detail about Hot Springs is that it is actually our oldest national park. In 1832, President Andrew Jackson signed a law setting aside "four sections of land including said (hot) springs, reserved for the future disposal of the United States (which) shall not be entered, located, or appropriated, for any other purpose whatsoever." It would be another forty years before Yellowstone became the second.

As you might guess, Hot Springs National Park is mostly about the water. In fact, the most popular thing to do is take a bath in the waters! So we did. We bought a package deal at our hotel for a massage and a soak, ready to immerse ourselves in the aforementioned hot springs, which have a sulfuric, rotten-eggs smell.

Nearly a year later, as I researched and wrote a magazine article about Hot Springs, I discovered that only a few spas use the mineral water from the springs—and the one we went to wasn't one of them! Our hotel didn't *say* it used the spring water; I just assumed it did. The places that *do* use the water from the hot springs, I found out, specifically let you know.

This discovery gave Mimi and me a good laugh, but it didn't bother us. We weren't looking for the healing and medicinal properties attributed to the thermal springs anyway. These days, doctors don't prescribe "taking the waters" as a cure like they used to. The Park Service explicitly makes no claims about either drinking or bathing in the water. I don't think we missed anything by not soaking in the real springs. Honestly, all we cared about was relaxing in water that was clean and hot!

I was reminded of our misunderstanding during a conversation I had at a writer's conference not long afterward. One of the women announced that nowhere in the Gospels—the New Testament books of Matthew, Mark, Luke, and John—did Jesus say he was God.

"Actually, he did, in John 10:30," I replied. Another then stated her opinion that what was spiritual truth for one person wasn't necessarily truth for someone else. "But how can there be more than one truth?" I asked. "Truth is, by definition, objective. Something is either true or it isn't. In addition to proclaiming his deity, Jesus said he is 'the way, the truth and the life' [John 14:6]. So either he is who he says he is, or he's a nut job and shouldn't be paid any attention to." (If you've read C. S. Lewis's *Mere Christianity*, you might recognize this line of reasoning.)

My words didn't go over very well, needless to say, and the three people who had invited me to their table quickly made excuses to go elsewhere. Obviously, when having the right information mattered, they were quite content dabbling in "water" of their own making. They were either ignorant of or indifferent to its source, and to the One who makes very specific, life altering claims, like this one from Jeremiah 2:13: "My people have committed two sins: They have forsaken me, the spring of living water, and have dug their own cisterns, broken cisterns that cannot hold water."

Sadly, I recognized that I'm also guilty of trying to do things my own way. Too often I carve out a personal reservoir of self-sufficiency, pouring in everything I find meaningful—work, family, friends — only to find that it's a leaky container, and I can't quite get enough. God never promised those things would satisfy me any more than the hotel said we were soaking in the official hot springs.

What God does guarantee is that his spring of living water never runs dry, and I only have to plunge back in to find relief. My prayer is that you too will accept no imitations, but soak, drink, and revel in the refreshing fountain of life that is the real deal.

See for Yourself

Hot Springs National Park: *www.nps.gov/hosp*

Buckstaff Baths and Quapaw Baths and Spa are good places to go for a soak, perhaps after you hike one of the myriad of trails in the park. There are eight historic bathhouse buildings, constructed between 1892 and 1923, and you can find them on Bathhouse Row, along with the Grand Promenade. Tour the pretty Fordyce Bathhouse, which is also the park's Visitor Center, and take a step back in time. And if you can stomach it, hold your nose and drink the water...

Easter Peace
Shiloh National Military Park

The scepter shall not depart from Judah, nor the ruler's staff from between his feet, until Shiloh comes.

Genesis 49:10

Shiloh, Tennessee is the scene of one of the Civil War's most bloodstained battles. Of the almost 110 thousand soldiers who clashed in early April 1862, there were 23,746 causalities. It's an astounding number by itself, made even more poignant by this fact: more men were killed, wounded, or missing from just this one Civil War skirmish than the United States had suffered in all of its previous conflicts combined.

The Union Army's aim was to sever Confederate transportation lines at this important junction where two railroads met. General Albert Sidney Johnston, supreme Confederate commander in the West, was to intercept Union Major General Ulysses S. Grant's army and protect the strategic location.

Johnston took a bullet in his right leg and bled to death from the wound, leaving General P. G. T. Beauregard in command. The following day, Major General Don Carlos Buell reinforced Grant's troops, and the combined forces pounded the Confederates. Beauregard withdrew his ranks to the nearby town of Corinth, Mississippi, and eventually had to move even further south as the Union soldiers continued to gain ground. All this fighting opened the door for Grant's campaign to reestablish Union control over the Mississippi River.

In the Bible, Shiloh has a couple of meanings. Joshua 18 mentions it as the place where the Israelites first set up the tent of meeting, the tabernacle. Within the tabernacle was, among other things, the Ark of the Covenant, which held the tablets of the Law given to Moses by God. Those tablets had been sprinkled with the blood of young bulls as a peace offering, a kind of ritual ratification of the agreement between God and the people.

Exodus chapters twenty-five through thirty-one detail God's instructions for the tabernacle's construction and contents, while chapters thirty-five through forty describe how the people carried them out. After all was done, "the glory of the Lord filled the tabernacle" (Exodus 40:34). With the tabernacle situated in Shiloh, that city became the nation of Israel's religious center, where God's presence and power resided.

In Genesis 49:10, Shiloh refers to a person, rather than a place. It's a Messianic title, "the one who brings peace," meaning Jesus, whose coming was foretold throughout the Old Testament. Other names given to him in the Scriptures confirm that designation: he is the

"Prince of Peace" (Isaiah 9:6), Yahweh Shalom in the flesh (Judges 6:24).

While the Biblical city of Shiloh fell into ruin and today is just a small Israeli settlement, the American Shiloh is a very serene place. The National Park Service calls it one of the Civil War's most pristine battlefields. On those long ago April days, however, it was anything but peaceful.

Jesus's first coming wasn't exactly peaceful either. "Do not suppose that I have come to bring peace to the earth," he warned in Matthew 10:34. "I did not come to bring peace, but a sword." He arrived on earth to do battle for our souls, facing fierce hostility and death on a cross. Three days later, on the day we now celebrate as Easter, he triumphed.

In our present day culture, Easter is considered a "nice" holiday. The weather usually is balmy, full of hope for warmer weather ahead. Bunnies and chicks, bright springtime colors, and lots of chocolate predominate.

But getting to that first Easter wasn't any prettier than the road to Shiloh, Tennessee.

The New Testament books of Matthew, Mark, Luke, and John present a grim picture of Jesus's trial and crucifixion. He was whipped, spat upon, and mocked, and suffered an agonizing death. Like those young bulls whose blood sealed the covenant in the tabernacle, Jesus needed to shed his blood to seal a new covenant. He was qualified to do so because God's presence and power resided in him. He came "through the greater and more perfect tabernacle that is not man-made [and] did not enter by means of the blood of goats and calves; but he entered the Most Holy Place once for all by his own blood, having obtained eternal redemption" (Hebrews 9:12). The struggle may have been hard, but the victory was decisive.

There awaits yet a final battle. When Jesus appears again, he will bring an end to all sorrow and pain, and usher in peace that will last eternally.

Six hundred twenty thousand people gave up their lives during the Civil War. That was the price of preserving the Union, of making peace. It took just one Man to bring us our Shiloh.

Something to rejoice in, at not only Easter, but every day of the year.

See for Yourself

Shiloh National Military Park: *www.nps.gov/shil*

View the film "Shiloh: Fiery Trail" and check out the exhibits at the Shiloh Battlefield Visitor Center, then take a self-guided auto tour of the site. Special events are held every April 6 and 7, the actual dates of battle, and daily ranger-led programs are scheduled from Memorial Day through Labor Day. At its Corinth, Mississippi locale, the park features two other movies, exhibits, and car and walking tours.

He's Alive!
Mount Rushmore National Memorial

In my former book, Theophilus, I wrote about all that Jesus began to do and to teach until the day he was taken up to heaven, after giving instructions through the Holy Spirit to the apostles he had chosen. After his suffering, he showed himself to these men and gave many convincing proofs that he was alive. He appeared to them over a period of forty days and spoke about the kingdom of God.

Acts 1:1-3

Ever wonder how the faces of four presidents came to be carved in the Black Hills of South Dakota?

As is often the case with tourist attractions, Mount Rushmore National Memorial got its start with a man who wanted people from all over the country to visit his state. In 1924, Doane Robinson, South Dakota's state historian, contacted Gutzon Borglum with his idea of giant statues, as the sculptor worked on the face of Confederate General Robert E. Lee at Georgia's Stone Mountain.

Borglum took him up on the challenge. Two scouting trips later, he settled on the location of Mount Rushmore, named for New York City lawyer Charles E. Rushmore, who had spent time with prospectors in the Hills. Two South Dakota congressmen pushed for federal and state approval, and President Calvin Coolidge's presence at the mountain's initial dedication helped secure the legislation and United States Treasury funding. The work began in 1927 and continued for fourteen years. In 1933, the project came under the jurisdiction of the National Park Service.

Borglum didn't live to see the completion of Mount Rushmore. He died in early 1941, seven months before the memorial's dedication in October. His son Lincoln handled the finishing touches.

The sixty-foot granite heads of Presidents Washington, Jefferson, Lincoln, and Theodore Roosevelt were Borglum's final works, but he's known for many others. His *Mares of Diomedes* was the first piece of American sculpture bought for New York's Metropolitan Museum of Art. He produced angelic statues for the city's Cathedral of Saint John the Divine, made Washington, D.C.'s large equestrian bronze of General Philip Sheridan, and created a memorial to Pickett's Charge on the Gettysburg battlefield (the latter two are both located in National Park sites). In Newark, New Jersey, his *Wars of America*, a huge memorial with forty-two humans and two horses, is set in downtown Military Park, and *Seated Lincoln* graces the county courthouse.

But Mount Rushmore remains Borglum's most noted accomplishment. "This is no mere 'colossal' stunt," he said of the massive undertaking. "I am simply animating the mountain."

The word "animate" comes from Latin verb *animare*, meaning, "to give life to." Every Easter we celebrate that Jesus is "animated," or made alive. It's no "colossal stunt," even though many have tried to make it out to be. The chief priests and the elders conspired to cover up the fantastic truth when word of the empty tomb reached them. "They gave the soldiers [who had guarded Jesus's grave] a large sum of money, telling them, 'You are to say, "His disciples stole him away while we were asleep." If this report gets to the governor, we will satisfy him and keep you out of trouble.' So the soldiers took the money and did as they were instructed" (Matthew 28:12-15).

This story, of course, has so many contradictions it's laughable. How could sleeping people know what happened? Would it be likely all the soldiers were sleeping at the same time? Would they risk incriminating themselves even for a large bribe?

The Gospels and Luke's second letter, the book of Acts, record several instances of Jesus showing himself alive to his followers. The apostle Paul testified that Jesus appeared to more than five hundred people at one time, with living witnesses still attesting to that fact twenty-five years later. As the apostle Peter avows, "We did not follow cleverly invented stories when we told you about the power and coming of our Lord Jesus Christ, but we were eyewitnesses of his majesty" (2 Peter 1:16).

Experiencing Mount Rushmore is awesome, especially at night, when the Park Service puts on a spectacular light show. But knowing the "Living One [who is] alive forever and ever" (Revelation 1:18)—indescribable!

See for Yourself

Mount Rushmore National Memorial: *www.nps.gov/moru*

You can walk up the short but steep Presidential Trail—.6 miles long, 422 stairs—behind the immense stone carvings of the four presidents. No, you won't see their backsides, as a cartoon I've seen depicts!

Spoiler alerts ahead: the climactic finale of Alfred Hitchcock's *North by Northwest* is set at Mount Rushmore. If you look carefully at the scene in the park's cafeteria, just before Eva Marie Saint shoots Cary Grant, off to the side you'll see a young boy screw up his face in anticipation of the prop gun's loud bang.

While you're in the area, consider side trips to four other nearby National Park locations: Jewel Cave National Monument, Wind Cave and Badlands National Parks, and the Minuteman Missile National Historic Site. Save money with an annual pass that covers entrance fees for all occupants of a personal vehicle to these parks and more than two thousand other federal recreation sites. Children age fifteen and under are always admitted free. A Senior Pass is a low-cost bargain, allowing those sixty-two and older to get into parks free—for life!

The best bargain, though, is in April. National Park Week brings a whole seven days of free entrance to all national park sites.

Are we just doing things for show? What are we actually accomplishing?

Things we sacrifice for/invest in are often the things that make us slaves to them.

More Precious Than Silver, More Costly Than Gold
Golden Spike National Historic Site

> *All who make idols are nothing, and the things they treasure are worthless.*
>
> Isaiah 44:9

A national park site named for a nail? Seems funny, doesn't it? But it's not just any old piece of hardware: Utah's Golden Spike National Historic Site celebrates the completion of the first Transcontinental Railroad, when the Union Pacific and Central Pacific Railroads linked up. This rail line was a big deal because it cut the time of a coast-to-coast trip from months to days, ushering in the era of America's westward expansion.

The Central Pacific Railroad began laying track heading east from Sacramento, California in 1863, using primarily Chinese immigrants as laborers. That same year, the Union Pacific Railroad worked westward from Omaha, Nebraska, employing many workers from Ireland. Both groups toiled under difficult and often dangerous conditions, sometimes putting in fifteen-hour days in a race to see who could put down the most rails. The Irish had the easier job; those blasting through the rugged Sierra Nevada mountain range faced a tougher task. The two sections finally connected at Promontory Summit in northern Utah in May 1869.

On the tenth of that month, a ceremony took place to officially mark the joining of the lines. A San Francisco contractor felt there should be a commemorative item for the occasion, so using about $400 worth of his own precious metal, he had a golden spike cast.

A San Francisco newspaper owner ordered a second gold spike, while a gubernatorial candidate for the new state of Nevada had one forged in silver. Arizona Territory's governor also commissioned a spike, made up of both gold and silver. Other equipment manufactured to join the tracks included a laurel wood tie into which the spikes would be driven and a silver maul, or spike hammer, with which to do the deed.

All of these pieces, of course, were just for show. Central Pacific President Leland Stanford and Union Pacific Vice-President Thomas Durant merely tapped the spikes, leaving all the instruments preserved for posterity without any marks.

Then three ordinary iron spikes, an iron maul, and a basic pine tie replaced the commemorative items. Stanford swung at the spike and hit the tie; Durant took a turn and missed even the tie. It fell to a regular rail worker to actually drive home that last spike.

What became of those ceremonial pieces? The gold and the silver spikes as well as the silver maul now reside at the Cantor Arts Museum at Stanford University, named after you-know-who. The

Museum of the City of New York owns the gold and silver spike that was commissioned by the Arizona Territory governor. The specially crafted tie ended up in the San Francisco offices of the Southern Pacific (the Central Pacific Railroad became Southern Pacific) and burnt during that city's 1906 earthquake and fire. The silver spike's location is unknown, but it's speculated that it too might have been in San Francisco and suffered the same fate.

I understand the symbolic importance of these articles—constructing a railroad that stretched from ocean to ocean was a great accomplishment that changed the United States, and seeing them helps us remember that achievement. Yet, on that day so long ago, they were essentially worthless. They were useless to do the actual job of joining two railroad tracks.

We humans have a tendency to build, care for, and assign value to things that have no real, practical value. As the prophet Isaiah noted, the things we sacrifice for, invest in, and count as precious—possessions, careers, successes—often make us their slaves, drive us to distraction, and catch us up in an endless cycle of futility. We try to make our "gold and silver" into what they were never meant to be.

We should definitely celebrate achievements. Without men and women of vision, and the workers who carry out their plans, our country would be a mere shadow of itself. But great exploits will never completely fulfill us; there's always more to accomplish. "Yet when I surveyed all that my hands had done and what I had toiled to achieve," King Solomon bemoaned in Ecclesiastes 2:11, "Everything was meaningless, a chasing after the wind; nothing was gained under the sun."

So how are we to find a happy medium? Solomon concludes, "A man can do nothing better than to eat and drink and find satisfaction in his work. This too, I see, is from the hand of God, for without him, who can eat or find enjoyment?" (v. 24).

That is exactly the lasting alternative the Lord offers: "Why spend money on what is not bread, and your labor on what does not satisfy? Listen, listen to me, and eat what is good, and your soul will delight in the richest of fare. Give ear and come to me; hear me, that your soul may live" (Isaiah 55:2-3).

And no hammer blows, no fire, nor anything else can take that away from us.

See for Yourself

Golden Spike National Historical Site: *www.nps.gov/gosp*

The park consists of 2,735 acres of land surrounding a fifteen-mile stretch of the original Transcontinental Railroad. There's only one paved road to the site, located in a remote valley on the north end of the Great Salt Lake. GPS units might send you to the wrong spot—check the park's website for accurate directions.

Every May 10, Golden Spike NHS conducts a ceremonial reenactment, which is repeated twice daily every Saturday and holiday through mid-September. While you're there, walk a trail or take a self-guided auto tour to spot traces of track construction. Replica locomotives from days gone by are on display in the Engine House during the winter.

Firsts and Lasts
De Soto National Monument

*I am the Alpha and the Omega, the First and the Last, the Beginning
and the End.*

Revelation 22:13

Hernando de Soto was a man of firsts. He and his troops were the
first Europeans to move far into the North American continent, first
whites to reconnoiter the Mississippi River above its estuary, and
among the first to encounter Native Americans. Yet his mission wasn't
original at all. Like explorers before him, his ultimate quest was fame
and fortune.

De Soto began his career as a soldier eager to find treasure and glory
in the New World, rumored to hold vast riches in its verdant lands.
He left Spain at age fourteen to raid present-day Central America,
raking in huge profits from gold and slaves. Then he linked up with
fellow Spaniard Francisco Pizarro to take over Peru.

After twenty-two years, he returned home a wealthy man, but soon became restless and bored. He struck a deal with Charles V to canvass and colonize "La Florida" using his own funds, with the Spanish king receiving one-fifth of the cache taken in battle or trade, and half from grave and temple plundering. As a reward, de Soto could divvy up the rest of the loot with his crew, and become governor of Cuba and the new colony.

On May 30, 1539, de Soto and his party landed on Florida's west coast, probably near Tampa Bay, the locale now set aside as De Soto National Monument. Over the next four years, the men covered some four thousand miles throughout what is today's southeastern United States.

The journey was not a happy one for de Soto's party or for the natives they encountered. The expedition was dependent upon the Indians for food and help, and when they didn't get what they wanted, they took it anyway, usually by force. De Soto captured Indian men and women and made them work as slaves. The group similarly appropriated horses, weapons, and supplies. All for nothing.

Hostile inhabitants, unfamiliar territory, and de Soto's fanatical pursuit of gold and silver eventually doomed the expedition. He never found precious metals and never established colonies. De Soto's trail of disease, death, and destruction ended with his own demise from fever. He was buried in the Mississippi River so the Native Americans wouldn't know he wasn't the immortal he claimed to be. Sixteen months later, his army's ragtag remnants withdrew to Mexico.

Contrast this conquistador with Jesus, another man of firsts. In Colossians 1:15-17, he is called the firstborn over all creation, with control over everything. First Corinthians 15:20-23 also likens Jesus to the "firstfruits" offering mentioned in Leviticus 23:9-14.

God's people celebrated the firstfruits ceremony, detailed in Deuteronomy 26:1-11, on the second day of the Feast of Unleavened Bread as a time of thanksgiving. They presented a sheaf of barley to the Lord in acknowledgement of his provision as well as to consecrate the entire grain crop to him, as a pledge of the full harvest to come. Jesus, raised from the dead, is our promise that the One who was there at the beginning will not only gather in all his followers, but also come again and take them home with him.

But here's the incredible thing—even though he was *numero uno*, Jesus assumed the lowest place. Unlike de Soto, he *knew* he was God, but purposely subjected himself to the most subordinate position of humanity—a sacrifice: "Being in very nature God, [he] did not consider equality with God something to be grasped, but made himself nothing, taking the very nature of a servant...he humbled himself and became obedient to death—even death on a cross!" (Philippians 2:6-8). He chose to take the first step toward us, doing what we could not do for ourselves, dying for us while we were still sinners. He didn't come to seek swag like de Soto hungered for. He came to seek people, not for enslavement but to set them free and to reveal himself as the real treasure.

Just as we would say we have things covered from A to Z, Jesus used the alphabet to emphasize his rule from the beginning of time until the end. Christ the firstfruits' resurrection from death and ascension into heaven is a pledge of his second coming and of his followers' rebirth into eternity: "For as in Adam all die, so in Christ all will be made alive. But each in his own turn: Christ, the firstfruits; then when he comes, those who belong to him. Then the end will come" (1 Corinthians 15:22-24).

In the meantime, he asks some firsts and lasts of us, to major in him while minoring in self. It's a tough balance. Jesus did it perfectly, but we fall woefully short, empowered and upheld only by his grace.

De Soto's body was never found. He remains dead and gone. By now no smidgen of him remains. That's because he indeed was a mere mortal.

We find no trace of Jesus's body either. And yet he is alive, testified to by hundreds. As Job recognized, despite his suffering, "I know that my Redeemer lives," he confidently asserted in Job 19:25, "and that in the end he will stand upon the earth." Job believed the Living God who is the same yesterday and today and forever, who was there at the very beginning, arranges the affairs of mankind now, and has the future all sewed up.

Our first, our last, and our greatest hope.

See for Yourself

De Soto National Monument: *www.nps.gov/deso*

A replica sixteenth-century native village opens on the monument grounds in Bradenton every year from December through April, Florida's prime tourist season. Costumed interpreters display and discuss period armor, weaponry, crafts, and talk about the expedition. This Living History Camp culminates in a reenactment of de Soto's landing, a popular day long event.

Fall and early spring bring flocks of migrating birds. The Visitor Center, open all year, shows an introductory film and displays artifacts from the de Soto era. Take a walk on the Memorial Trail any time to spot two unusual trees, mangroves with their funky root system and gumbo-limbos. The latter are also called "tourist trees," because their red bark peels like a sunburned vacationer.

The Unheeded Warning
Johnstown Flood National Memorial

For you know very well that the day of the Lord will come like a thief in the night. While people are saying, "Peace and safety," destruction will come on them suddenly, as labor pains on a pregnant woman, and they will not escape.

1 Thessalonians 5:2-3

May 31 marks the anniversary of one of the biggest stories of the nineteenth century. In a single day, 2,209 people perished, shocking the country, leading to an outpouring of national grief and support, and cementing the reputation of a newly formed but now well-known relief organization, the American Red Cross.

On that date in 1889, twenty million tons of water broke through the South Fork Dam and swept through the southwestern Pennsylvania town of Johnstown, leaving massive destruction and loss of life in its wake. The National Park Service commemorates the disaster at its National Memorial in the town, and every year on the evening of May 31 sets out 2,209 luminarias to honor the victims.

David McCullough's 1968 book, *The Johnstown Flood*, incorporates the accounts of witnesses and survivors, making his narrative one of the best written about the flood. McCullough sets the stage with what led up to the fateful day. Lake Conemaugh, fourteen miles upriver from Johnstown, was the pleasure lake of The South Fork Fishing and Hunting Club, formed by a group of prominent Pittsburgh businessmen. Club members included steel magnate Andrew Carnegie; millionaire entrepreneur Henry Clay Frick; Philander Chase Knox, United States Senator and holder of several Cabinet positions under different presidents; and banker Andrew Mellon, who later became Secretary of the Treasury during the Harding, Coolidge, and part of the Hoover administrations. Another member was John Fulton, general manager of Cambria Iron and Steel, who evaluated the dam holding back the lake in 1880 and found it to be an accident waiting to happen. Over the years, the club made numerous efforts to shore up the dam, but in reality, it was badly neglected. And the townspeople knew it.

Johnstown had a history of flooding, and with a torrential rainstorm pounding the town the last week of May 1889, residents were busy preparing to protect their property from the overflow of The Little Conemaugh and the Stony Creek Rivers, as they had in the past. At the dam, laborers worked frantically to add height and dig out a second spillway to relieve pressure from the lake's rapidly rising waters. The resident engineer even sent someone out to the nearest town of South Fork to notify those in the waters' path.

The warning was too little too late. Just after 3:00 p.m., the dam gave way. A train engineer saw the body of water rushing forward, and tied down his train whistle in a futile attempt to alert residents of the coming calamity. A wave estimated to have the force of Niagara Falls swept into Johnstown, becoming a rolling hill of debris approximately forty feet high and half a mile wide—leaving flood lines as high as eighty-nine feet above river level. The torrent carried houses, locomotives, and both dead and living animals and people as it tore through small communities on its journey from the dam. Survivors described the sound as a tremendous rumble.

The Pennsylvania Railroad Company's Stone Bridge at the other end of town trapped much of the wreckage. The debris, piled forty feet high, and spread over thirty acres, then caught fire. The floodwaters continued to sweep many victims down the Conemaugh River to their deaths, while the more fortunate were rescued at towns further downstream. Incredibly, bodies were found as far away as Cincinnati, Ohio, and as late as 1911. The catastrophe destroyed sixteen hundred homes and did $17 million (in 1889 dollars) in property damage, wiping out four square miles of downtown Johnstown.

Over $3.5 million, collected across the United States and eighteen foreign countries, aided survivors and helped rebuild the area. It became the first major peacetime disaster relief effort for the American Red Cross. The International Red Cross began in Europe as a battlefield relief organization. But Clara Barton, who organized the American branch in 1881, arrived with other workers just five days after the flood, certain that the Red Cross should help with other calamities.

Destruction. Distress. Death. The same words that apply to the Johnstown Flood are found in Biblical passages referring to the time when Jesus will come again. Although there will be general signs of his return, Scripture says no one except God knows when that will happen, even if many try to predict it. When Jesus actually does appear, there will be no mistake about it. Visual and auditory phenomena—a loud trumpet, lightning flashes across the sky, and Jesus bodily descending from the clouds—will make his second arrival obvious.

Until then, Jesus tells his followers to keep watch and stay alert. "As it was in the days of Noah, so it will be at the coming of the Son of Man," he counsels in Matthew 24:37-39. "For in the days before the flood, people were eating and drinking, marrying and giving in marriage, up to the day Noah entered the ark; and they knew nothing about what would happen until the flood came and took them all away."

Like the people of Johnstown, we too ignore the warnings. We react three ways.

First, we actively pursue our own agenda. Jesus tells a parable about a servant, put in charge of property while his boss was on a journey, who treats his fellow servants harshly and parties with abandon.

However, Jesus warns, "The master of that servant will come on a day when he does not expect him and at an hour he is not aware of. He will cut him to pieces and assign him a place with the hypocrites, where there will be weeping and gnashing of teeth" (Matthew 24:50-51).

Or we carry on with blissful oblivion. In another parable, a shortsighted rich man whose crops had done very well assumed that his amassed wealth was all he needed. "Take life easy; eat, drink and be merry," he told himself (Luke 12:19). What he hadn't made provision for was an abrupt summons to face God to account for his neglected and impoverished soul.

The final choice is to be ready. "Let us not be like others who are asleep, but let us be alert and self-controlled...For God did not appoint us to suffer wrath but to receive salvation through our Lord Jesus Christ," adjures the apostle Paul. "He died for us so that we may live together with him" (1 Thessalonians 5:6, 9-10).

Maybe you don't believe the dam ever will break, that Jesus won't come again to judge the world based on our faith in him. Perhaps you don't even believe there is a God. You might think this is all hysterical talk and a bunch of nonsense. You'll just take your chances on what happens in the next life—if there is one. That's your prerogative; God never forces anyone to believe.

Yet, the engineers at the South Fork Dam and on the train saw it as their duty to sound the alarm about the coming flood, hoping to spare at least some. I would be remiss if I failed to do the same.

See for Yourself

Johnstown Flood National Memorial: *www.nps.gov/jofl*

This park is about seventy miles east of Pittsburgh, Pennsylvania and is open year round. First, stop by the Visitor Center to watch the film "Black Friday." Then take a guided path-of-the-flood van or hiking tour, offered at various times June through September, with reservations required.

[Handwritten note at top: Jesus doesn't dim down the cost/sacrifice of becoming a christian. It's a hard, narrow path but God equips us for every battle we face. We are/never will be never abandoned or abandoned or left on our own.]

Worth It?

Great Smoky Mountains National Park

*Suppose one of you wants to build a tower. Will he not first sit down
and estimate the cost to see if he has enough money to complete it?*

Luke 14:28

May 22 marks the anniversary of Great Smoky Mountains National
Park, which straddles the Tennessee-North Carolina border.

As its website notes, "Becoming a national park was not easy for the
Great Smokies." Older parks, located in the western United States,
had been carved out of land already owned by the government, "often
places where no one wanted to live anyway." But in this region of the
country, the land was owned by "hundreds of small farmers and a
handful of large timber and paper companies [who] did not want to
leave their family homesteads [or] abandon huge forests of timber,
many miles of railroad track, extensive systems of logging equipment,
and whole villages of employee housing."

Others, though, had wanted to set aside land in the Appalachians as either a national park or national forest for years. It wasn't until the rising popularity of the automobile in the 1920s that the push for accessibility through the beautiful scenery forced the issue to a head. In 1926 President Calvin Coolidge signed a bill that provided for the establishment of the Great Smoky Mountains National Park.

There remained one snag. One hundred fifty thousand acres had to be purchased, and the federal government wasn't permitted to do that. So the state legislatures of North Carolina and Tennessee each appropriated $2 million. Money given by private groups, individuals, and schoolchildren who contributed their pennies brought the total up to $5 million. A matching contribution from the Laura Spellman Rockefeller Memorial Fund provided the final funds.

Then came the hardest part—wresting the land from the original owners. As you might imagine, some people and companies were glad for the money—especially since the country was by then in the middle of the Depression—but others felt sad or angry to lose their homes.

Dedication to a cause involves persistence and effort, and can bring strife and hardship to everyone affected, even if the results are for the benefit of many more. There's a price to be paid, financial and/or otherwise. What's easy to subscribe to in principle becomes daunting when it's time for action.

Jesus doesn't shy away from asking his followers to consider what it will cost to follow him, to contemplate what it takes to commit their lives to his control. Scrutiny doesn't intimidate him; on the contrary, he invites it. He knows he's "the way and the truth and the life" (John 14:6), so he's untroubled as to whether he'll stand up under the analysis.

But Jesus lets it be known that his way means a life of sacrifice and denial. Negating or sugar coating the struggle is false advertising, quite frankly, and he will have none of it. Jesus is up front about the discipline it takes to gamely station ourselves between the two forces who battle for our souls, the Prince of Peace and the "ruler of the kingdom of the air" (Ephesians 2:2), called Satan. "Suppose a king is about to go to war against another king. Will he not first sit down and consider whether he is able with ten thousand men to oppose the one coming against him with twenty thousand?" (Luke 14:31). I like the way G. K. Chesterton put it in his 1912 book, *What's Wrong with the World*: "The Christian ideal has not been tried and found wanting. It has been found difficult; and left untried."

Jesus calls the entire world, from the one-percenters to the down-and-outers. His kingdom isn't a closed and exclusive society. Yet he also knows who will respond in the affirmative. The self-reliant and the indifferent invitees take one whiff of what's required—a will centered not on ego but on God—and give it up as too much effort. Those who do sign on to living God's way must be ready for the challenge.

The great news is that we're not left alone or unprepared for combat. The Lord is always with us, fighting on our behalf. He equips us as the need arises. He knows we feeble and inconsistent disciples need incentives to keep us going, and he freely and unabashedly promises them: "Anyone who comes to him must believe that he exists and that he rewards those who earnestly seek him" (Hebrews 11:6).

Determination, sacrifice, sweat, and undoubtedly, tears went into making the Smokies a park. Many paid the price for the sake of the greater good. The result is pleasure and enjoyment for the millions who visit it every year. Most would say the cost was worth it.

Such is the Christian life. Jesus bought us not with money but with himself, also with determination, sacrifice, and yes, tears. Though he was God in the flesh, he didn't lord his exalted position over others nor turn an unsympathetic ear to his creation. Instead he "died for sins once for all, the righteous for the unrighteous, to bring [us] to God" (1 Peter 2:18).

The result is the greater good for him as well as for us. "Worthy is the Lamb, who was slain, to receive power and wealth and wisdom and strength and honor and glory and praise!" the heavenly beings in Revelation 5:12 proclaim at the end of time.

Worth it? You bet!

See for Yourself

Great Smoky Mountains National Park: *www.nps.gov/grsm*

Because of its location in the heavily populated eastern part of the country, this park welcomes more visitors than any other unit of the Park Service, so make reservations ahead of arriving. And since park elevations range from around 900 to 6,643 feet, be sure to take the right clothing. Tenters and RVers can choose among ten campgrounds, but the lone lodge within the park is accessible only by hiking to the summit of Mt. Le Conte. Food and beverage services also are limited. Not to worry though, the nearby towns of Gatlinburg, Pigeon Forge, and Sevierville, Tennessee have sufficient places to stay and eat.

The more than twelve hundred people who had to vacate their land left behind many buildings. Over seventy of them remain; the park has the largest collection of historic log structures in the East.

Waterfalls also are abundant in the Smokies. For a bit of a challenge in the spring when snowmelt swells the streams, park at the Visitor Center at the Great Smoky Mountains Institute at Tremont, then hike up the service road to a trailhead, or follow the Lumber Ridge Trail to the Buckeye Trail. The approximately two-mile round trip path is rocky and steep in places, but the reward is seeing the multitiered Spruce Flats Falls.

Summer

Every Day Should Be Memorial Day
Acadia National Park

These stones are to be a memorial to the people of Israel forever.

Joshua 4:7

How many of us pick up appealing or unusual stones we spot along a path or shoreline to save as souvenirs?

Count me among those who do that and think nothing of it. But in the national parks, it's illegal.

At Maine's Acadia National Park, rock stealing is a besetting problem. Signs instruct visitors not to remove stones, but they take them anyway. Rangers have spotted people with pockets and backpacks bulging with rocks, and have even seen some tossing slabs into their cars.

The theft of natural resources from federal lands has always been an issue. The punishment for pilfering, a misdemeanor, can range from a mere warning to a maximum fine of $5,000 and six months in jail. But it seems Acadia's water-smoothed stones from its lakes and seashores are especially tempting to take away as a remembrance.

God also used rocks to remind his people of not only where they'd been but also how they got there. Joshua chapter three relates how God held back the Jordan River so the Israelites, bearing the Ark of the Covenant, could cross into the Promised Land on dry ground.

To commemorate this miracle, God commanded Joshua to choose one man from each of Israel's twelve tribes to pick a stone from the middle of the river, and haul it to where they were to camp that night, in Gilgal. God also directed Joshua to take up twelve more river stones and set them up in the riverbed where the priests who carried the ark stood. Then he arranged a cairn on dry land from the stones the others had gathered.

These two memorials stood as a testimony to the living and powerful God, the One who worked continuously on their behalf. For it was exactly forty years from the day the previous generation had escaped their bondage in Egypt, also by God's miraculous parting of water, in this case the Red Sea.

In the United States, Memorial Day weekend technically belongs in the spring, but it's the unofficial kick-off to summer. Formerly known as Decoration Day and originally set on May 30, the holiday began after the Civil War to remember the Union and Confederate soldiers who gave their lives. Eventually it became a day to honor the dead from every American war, not to be confused with Veteran's Day, observed in November, which pays homage to all who have served in the armed forces—living or dead.

These days we tend to mark Memorial Day with barbeques, family, and heavily advertised sales. But the occasion is so much more than that. It's a time of reflection, to acknowledge what has been done for us that we couldn't do for ourselves: secure our freedom. We as a nation need that reminder, so we don't forget those who gave the ultimate sacrifice.

Isn't that what these two biblical memorials erected by the Israelites stand for as well? Crossing the dry Jordan brought them freedom from Egyptian slavery.

While I don't advocate taking rocks or anything else from the parks, I do believe in creating memorials in tangible ways with journals, scrapbooks, and letters, as well as in daily words and deeds. I deeply appreciate those memorials handed down to me, and I want to leave my descendants a witness of the liberty the Lord has brought me.

What about you? What "stones" are you leaving behind so future generations can praise and thank God for his mighty works on behalf of his people?

They won't know unless you tell them.

See for Yourself

Acadia National Park: *www.nps.gov/acad*

Acadia's forty-five miles of carriage roads are a gift from philanthropist John D. Rockefeller and his family, and they enable visitors to drive, bike, and ride horses throughout the park. Free shuttles are available late June through Columbus Day in October.

A must see is Cadillac Mountain, the tallest peak on the East Coast. It's the first place in the country to see the sunrise in fall and winter.

There are three campgrounds in the park: two open only May to September or October, with limited sites available during the colder months. Seasonal reservations go fast, since the park gets more than two million visitors annually. Other lodging is available in nearby towns.

Jordan Pond House is the only place to purchase food in the park. Pick up a box lunch to eat as you explore Acadia, and treat yourself to its famous popovers at afternoon tea.

Lost and Found
Glacier National Park

For the Son of Man came to seek and to save what was lost.

Luke 19:10

Four family members and I traveled one summer to Glacier National Park near Kalispell, Montana, and experienced weather we didn't expect: it snowed.

My brother provided a bit of drama on that trip. We'd driven the awe-inspiring Going-to-the-Sun Road, which crosses the Continental Divide, climbing to Logan's Pass at 6,640 feet on an overcast and blustery day. We squeezed into the Visitor Center along with many others, and kept getting separated, as one of us would lag behind to look at an exhibit (that would be me), another went outside to take in the view, and somebody else went to the restroom. We all managed to finally find each other—except for my brother.

We couldn't locate that boy anywhere. My husband checked the men's room and I scoured the parking lot. My sister-in-law looked in and around the building. Mom huddled against the wind in a thin sweater next to the car, unable to get in because guess who had the key?

You know how it goes when you're looking for someone: first you're puzzled, then annoyed, then worried. Unfortunately a hiker had gone missing the week before we arrived, and flyers with his name, photo, description, and last known whereabouts were posted everywhere. When we couldn't find my brother, we females, who admittedly have very vivid imaginations and were perhaps influenced by seeing the flyer wherever we went, started voicing awful scenarios. What if he fell off a cliff? Could a wild animal have gotten to him? What if he's hurt and in a place where no one can see him? We joined Mom by the car and scared ourselves silly.

After what seemed like forever, out came my brother from the direction of the Visitor Center. "Where have you been?" we all asked, relieved but a little angry too.

"I was looking for you guys, and I thought I saw two of you on the trail, so I followed," he answered. "After a while, I realized it wasn't you, and came back."

My sister-in-law had the final word. "I was just beginning to wonder if I had a recent picture of you, because I was sure we were going to have to create a poster!"

Jesus drew on common experiences like this to illustrate spiritual truths, and he used the concept of loss in three parables in Luke 15: a shepherd hunts for a wayward animal, a woman sweeps her floor to find missing change, and a father watches for his rebellious son's return.

Did the sheep sense it was lost? Possibly. Maybe it got stuck somewhere and pitifully bleated until rescued. The money obviously had no clue it was misplaced. What about the Prodigal Son? I doubt he thought he'd gone astray, or if he did, he pushed the idea out of his mind. He was too busy living it up. It wasn't until he sank as low as he could get that he came to his senses.

And you? Which lost thing are you? Are you a sheep, following the wrong people on the wrong path, wandering from the One who calls himself the Good Shepherd, and not sure how to get back? Are you the coin, blissfully unaware you're mislaid, quite content to stay in the dirt, not realizing how valuable you are to God? Or are you the son, determined to do things your own way, no matter whom you hurt, yourself included?

Maybe like me you've been all three at one time or another. So let me tell you, in case you didn't know or need a reminder: God has made it his mission to find you. Everything about you is imprinted on his mind. And he's not going to be mad when you come back—quite the contrary. He's waiting to throw a party!

We never did discover if that vanished hiker was located. I suspect not, since too much time had passed without a sighting. My prayer is that if you feel lost in relation to God, you won't wait another moment to let him know you're ready to be found.

He's already initiated the search.

See for Yourself

Glacier National Park: www.nps.gov/glac

Like most western parks, Glacier is dramatically scenic. Save yourself the hassle of driving and instead hop aboard the free shuttle bus July 1 through Labor Day as it climbs Going-to-the-Sun Road—it's less dangerous than trying to steer and sightsee at the same time.

There's so much to do and the park is so big that you can easily become overwhelmed, so the website has suggestions for different itineraries. Try a cruise on St. Mary or Two Medicine Lake, and go hiking on trails ranging in difficulty from easy to strenuous. You'll find beautiful flora and fauna and spectacular views no matter where you go.

A fun day trip is to the bordering Canadian park of Waterton, which along with Glacier, forms Waterton-Glacier International Peace Park. If you go, be sure to bring your passport.

Here's a hint on accommodations: the rustic Lake McDonald Lodge is the park's least expensive lodging, but it has the best view of all. Ask for a lakeside room and experience a gorgeous vista every time you open your door. And at least peek into the Many Glacier Hotel to admire its grand lobby and dining room.

Our Defense
Golden Gate National Recreation Area
Minuteman Missile National Historic Site

The Lord is my light and my salvation—whom shall I fear? The Lord is the stronghold of my life—of whom shall I be afraid?

Psalm 27:1

From the mid-1950s through the '70s, Nike missiles were considered the United States' strongest bastion of defense. Over two hundred bases were arrayed in so-called "rings of steel" around major metropolitan areas and military bases during this period of time known as the Cold War, when guarding against an air attack by the USSR was America's top security priority.

First came the Nike Ajax, the initial surface-to-air missile (SAM) developed by the Army, a projectile that moved at more than twice the speed of sound and could take out a single target. Nike Hercules, the more potent second-generation SAM, contained a nuclear warhead.

As technology advanced, the Soviet threat shifted from planes to that of long-range intercontinental ballistic missiles (ICBMs). The Air Force developed our own country's nuclear ICBMs: the Atlas, Titan, and Minuteman series. Peacekeeper ICBMs came last.

The National Park Service exhibits Nikes in three locations: along the New Jersey shore at Gateway National Recreation Area's Sandy Hook unit, in southern Florida's Everglades National Park, and at Golden Gate National Recreation Area near San Francisco. South Dakota is home to the only Park Service unit specifically devoted to the Cold War, and it has, among other things, a Minuteman II training missile. In case you're wondering, all display rockets are disarmed.

You can find remnants of other old Nike bases scattered around the country—the information is readily available online. My husband and I went on a hunt for New Jersey's former Nike sites when I wrote an article about Sandy Hook, and we found them easily. Four hundred and fifty Minuteman III missiles remain in place across the Great Plains, each equipped with a single warhead.

What amazes me is that while the military tried to be as hush-hush as they could about the weapons, the Nikes weren't set in the middle of nowhere, but near cities and houses. People were somewhat aware of them. The Minutemen weapons were situated in more rural areas, but most locals knew something of what was going on. Numerous residents appreciated the economic benefits brought by an influx of soldiers and their families, and experienced a sense of patriotism while welcoming the additional security. Others felt less sure, wondering if the nearby missiles put them in greater danger. Probably only a few fully grasped how great a force sat in their backyards.

I've been to all four of these Park Service missile sites, most recently to the Golden Gate location. It has by far the best display of Nike missiles, and I was in awe as I witnessed one being raised out of the ground and tilted up as if it were about to take off. As a kid growing up during those days of "duck and cover" drills and the Cuban Missile Crisis, I remember the air of suspicion between the United States and the Communists, and the vaguely uneasy feeling that "something" could happen at any moment.

Things haven't changed that much, have they? That sense that the world could go blooey at the drop of a hat has never gone away—only the players are different. Today we worry about the Middle East and the tension both inside and among the countries in that region, as well as between them and us. The menace of another terrorist attack against the United States always looms.

Isn't it the same for us on a personal level too? An unexpected illness, a sudden financial crisis, a family emergency—all can occur in a split second (and may be happening to you now).

King David knew a lot about warfare, within and without his nation, his family, and himself. The Old Testament books of 1 Samuel (chapters 16 on) and 2 Samuel detail his highs and lows—the attempts on his life, the treacherous circumstances in which he often found himself, his rebellious household, and his willing participation in adultery and murder. Even this leader whom God called a man after his own heart had to remind himself to not be afraid.

I think of Psalm 27 as a combination of praise, a cry for help, and a pep talk, best summed up in verse three: "Though an army besiege me, my heart will not fear; though war break out against me, even then will I be confident."

The United States deactivated the Nike missile bases in the '70s because of the Strategic Arms Limitation Talks with the USSR. The Cold War era ended with the Soviet Union's collapse in the early '90s. The 1991 Strategic Arms Reduction Treaty led to the Minutemen II's retirement, and Peacekeepers lasted until the mid-2000s.

Our Savior, though, is the same yesterday, today, and forever. For the child of God, hope lies not in armaments or treaties but in the world's most powerful Warrior, an ever-present help in times of trouble, the one who overcame our greatest fear—death. Because he is Lord of all, we can rest easy no matter what enemy we face.

See for Yourself

Golden Gate National Recreation Area: *www.nps.gov/goga*

This urban park has so many different sections that it could take several days to see everything. Here are a few suggestions:

- Rent a bike at one of the numerous shops near San Francisco's Fisherman's Wharf and ride through the Presidio, an often-hilly meander through green space dotted with forts, parade grounds, and museums. You can even stay overnight at a hotel transformed from officers' quarters. Or just keep to the waterfront—the views are still great. The Crissy Field Warming Hut is a good place to grab lunch. If you're feeling adventurous, pedal across the Golden

Gate Bridge. Too tired to make the round trip? No shame in taking the Sausalito ferry back instead.

- Check out the Nike site in the Marin Headlands section, across the Golden Gate Bridge. It is only open Thursdays through Saturdays from 12:30 to 3:30 p.m. You can drive or take San Francisco Muni bus 76X to the Visitor Center on Saturdays. From there it's a short (uphill) walk to the missiles; further along is the Point Bonita Lighthouse.

Minuteman Missile National Historic Site: *www.nps.gov/mimi*

If you're going to Badlands National Park or Mount Rushmore in western South Dakota, consider a side trip here to learn more about America's Cold War defense.

Rescue
Gateway National Recreation Area

Rescue those being led away to death; hold back those staggering toward slaughter. If you say, "But we knew nothing about this," does not he who weighs the heart perceive it? Does not he who guards your life know it? Will he not repay each person according to what he has done?

Proverbs 24:11, 12

Gateway National Recreation Area spans twenty-seven thousand acres in a trio of areas over two states: Jamaica Bay and Staten Island in New York, and Sandy Hook, New Jersey. It's a diverse park serving a diverse urban population.

At the Sandy Hook Unit, I learned about the United States Life-Saving Service (USLSS). New Jersey has the most surviving USLSS stations in the country, and the one at Spermaceti Cove became Sandy Hook's Visitor Center before the aptly named Hurricane Sandy damaged the building.

Volunteer teams made up of fishermen and others familiar with the waters had long kept watch over our nation's shores. But from 1871 to

1914 hired crews, known as surfmen, took over the job of patrolling the coasts for ships in peril. (In 1914 the organization became part of the Coast Guard.)

The stations in which the surfmen resided were positioned along the East Coast from Maine to North Carolina. Sandy Hook was one of the first locations because of its proximity to busy New York harbor and its dangerous shoals. Eventually stations were added along the Gulf and Pacific Coasts, the Great Lakes, and in Alaska.

According to Dennis L. Noble, retired Coast Guard senior chief and author of the book, *That Others Might Live: The United States Life-Saving Service, 1878-1915*, the USLSS had two ways of rescuing people from ships stranded near shore: by boat and by a sturdy rope stretching from beach to vessel. The service crafts were massive and heavy, self-bailing and self-righting, and pulled by twelve to eighteen-foot oars. They also could be equipped with sails for work further offshore.

When the water was too turbulent or the weather extremely foul, the surfmen used what's called a Lyle gun to propel a line from shore to the boat. A life car, looking something like a mini submarine and capable of holding eleven people, could be hauled back and forth over, through, or even under the water to pick up the stranded mariners. After the men climbed in and the top hatch was sealed, there was enough air to last three minutes. Writes Noble, "It is hard to envision eleven people crowding into the car's small compartment but, as one surfman put it, people 'in that extremity are not apt to stand on the order of their going.'"

Ultimately, a breeches buoy—a life preserver ring with short canvas pants attached—replaced the heavy and awkward life cars. A sailor could then step into the contraption and be pulled to safety along the line.

Beach patrols went out every night, no matter what the weather, putting in as much as five miles or more on foot. These "soldiers of the surf" and "storm warriors," two other designations given to them, hoisted lanterns high, scanning the dark ocean for signs of trouble, ears attuned to cries of distress. During the day, they trained relentlessly. A lookout also stood watch in the station's tower in daytime. And stand he did, because there were no seats in the tower, to preclude any slacking off.

As you might suppose, a surfman's job was strenuous and dangerous. The unofficial USLSS motto says it all: "You have to go out, but you don't have to come back." Certainly many surfmen didn't come back, but by 1915, they had saved more than 178 thousand people.

Did these men hope and pray nothing ever happened during their watch? Probably. Did any ever hesitate before taking on the roiling surf on a cold, pitch-black night? Possibly. It's one thing to do your duty, quite another to realize you might lose your own life in doing so.

I imagine their constant drills enabled them to operate on instinct, so that it was almost second nature to hop into the boat or ply the line in times of crisis. Their job was to rescue people. The surfmen probably didn't think much about what they had to do—they just did what they'd been taught.

So often we Christians forget that outside, and even within, our holy huddles of church, Bible study, and fellowship, there are foundering and perishing people. Our natural tendency is to douse our lights and close our ears to their cries. Occasionally we might extend a helping hand, but pushing out into the surf? That's time-consuming, difficult, and scary!

In our disregard or half-hearted attempts, we neglect the responsibility God has given to each of us who has hired on to serve him. Standing safely on shore while feigning ignorance and pretending not to hear is simply not an option.

Rescue takes commitment. For a Christian, that means serious and persistent study of Scripture, and prayer. We may ask, *What's my duty to the poor and the hurting, and how exactly do I carry it out? And how do I minister to others and still keep my own head above water, so to speak?* Continuous training is what empowers us to act.

Martyrs are what we call people who go out in Christ's name and lose their lives in the process. We admire them, but we sure don't want to share their fate. Yet just as the surfmen acknowledged, the obligation to go exists hand in hand with the willingness to give all.

As we daily move among the tide of humanity, Jesus calls us to pay attention to those who could use a lifeline. We're charged with introducing them to the perfect surfman, who "rescued us from the dominion of darkness and brought us into the kingdom of the Son he loves" (Colossians 1:13). He's the only one who has the will, the power, and the desire to carry us safely home.

See for Yourself

Gateway National Recreation Area: *www.nps.gov/gate*

Access to New York Harbor, America's largest port, plays a big role in what you'll see at Gateway's three divisions. Sandy Hook boasts our nation's oldest surviving lighthouse and exhibits on maritime history. The remnants of Fort Hancock and the former Nike missile base, both of which are open to the public, testify to its strategic defense mission.

The Jamaica Bay Unit spreads over the New York City boroughs of Queens and Brooklyn, and is home to the Park Service's only Wildlife Refuge, situated at a former landfill. Military facilities and fortifications are found there and at the Staten Island Unit, which has an osprey-nesting site. All provide places to hike, bike, boat, swim, and even surf.

Stepping Out in Faith
Guadalupe Mountains National Park

When Moses sent them to spy out the land of Canaan, he said, "Go up through the Negev and on up into the hill country. See what the land is like". . . So they went up and explored the land [and] gave Moses this account: "[I]t does flow with milk and honey!. . . But the people who live there are powerful, and the cities are fortified and very large". . . Then Caleb said, "We should go up and take possession of the land, for we can certainly do it." But the men who had gone up with him said, "We can't attack those people; they are stronger than we are." And they spread among the Israelites a bad report about the land they had explored.

Numbers 13:17-18, 21, 27-28, 30-32

The shortest visit I ever made to a national park was to Guadalupe Mountains, an eighty-six thousand-acre spread in West Texas along its border with New Mexico. My family was on a tour of parks in the Southwest, and somehow Guadalupe had escaped our attention. When we saw the sign for it along the highway, we decided to stop in and have a look.

And that's about all we did. We seemed to be the only ones there at the time, not surprising because the park gets a mere two hundred thousand visitors a year. As we gazed at the vast, wild expanse from the Visitor Center, we felt uninspired to do much of anything. The scrubby drab desert terrain of cacti, yuccas, and thorn bushes didn't exactly beckon to us—it seemed too inhospitable and harsh. We took a half-hearted walk down a loop trail, then turned back and headed to our car.

Too bad for us. I recently read an article about the park, and realized all we'd missed—red-tailed hawks and peregrine falcons; a hike to McKittrick Canyon, where desert gives way to beautiful forest; and a more strenuous hike up Guadalupe Peak for a spectacular view.

I imagine our initial response to Guadalupe must be similar to that of the Israelites sent to check out the land God had promised them. We concentrated on what we didn't see at first, instead of what possibilities lay beyond.

We let a lack of time and unwillingness to make the effort thwart what could have been a memorable visit. In much the same way, the spies Moses sent out, while acknowledging the land looked good, nonetheless decided that the battle for it would never succeed and were afraid of even trying.

But, you know, there's a reason why Guadalupe is a national park. As the park brochure says, it's a real piece of the Old West as it used to be, a place to reflect on the courage of the pioneers and understand what drew them to the wild, untamed parts of our country in the first place.

In Numbers 14:2-3, the Israelites wept and moaned in the Negev: "If only we had died in Egypt! Or in this desert wilderness! Why is the Lord bringing us to this land only to let us fall by the sword?"

By God's grace, two of the twelve Israelite scouts stood resolute before the assembled masses. In Numbers 14:7-9, Joshua and Caleb countered, "The land we passed through and explored is exceedingly good. If the Lord is pleased with us, he will lead us into that land, a land flowing with milk and honey, and will give it to us. Only do not rebel against the Lord. And do not be afraid of the people of the land, because we will devour them. Their protection is gone, but the Lord is with us. Do not be afraid of them." The people's response was to consider stoning the obviously deluded pair of optimists.

Regrettably, the Israelites' lack of belief in God's assurances and his previous miracles of protection resulted in terrible consequences. Although they were at the edge of the Promised Land, they were forced to turn back into the wilderness, where they would wander for forty years. Those Israelites twenty years of age and older would die, except for Caleb and Joshua.

How often I also fail to move forward with what God's calling me to do because of fear! You too, I imagine. We come up with a multitude of excuses, asking ourselves, *What if I'm not up to the task? What if things don't turn out the way I want? What if I—gulp—fail?* We whine, *It's too hard! I'm too old!* What we often forget are the past instances of God's protection and leading, the inner reward we experience from doing what's right and best, and his promise of always being with us.

His presence enables us to be bold and step out into the seemingly inhospitable, barren wilderness he's brought us to, even when we're hesitant and uncertain. We might be uncomfortable and lonely at times, work like mad, and face scary obstacles. But the returns are much greater than if we play it safe.

When doubt and anxiety rear their ugly heads, we can remember the two faithful spies. Caleb, in one of his last Scriptural mentions (Joshua 14:6-14), was a vigorous eighty-five year old still ready to do battle for the Lord. Joshua became Moses' successor and went on to finally lead the next generation of Israelites into the Promised Land, as detailed in the book of Joshua. He's a prime example of faith, courage, obedience, and devotion to God—yet even *he* needed reassurance along the way.

So take heart, fellow wanderer! You'll find the same God accompanying you on your journey.

See for Yourself

Guadalupe Mountains National Park: *www.nps.gov/gumo*

Hiking and backpacking are popular activities in this spot situated 110 miles east of El Paso and fifty-six miles southwest of Carlsbad, New Mexico. Over eighty miles of trails include the forested Dog's Canyon and the two thousand-acre Salt Basin Dunes, a barren yet oddly picturesque area carved by wind. Caves within the park are inscribed with pictographs from the Mescalero Apaches who once roamed the area. There are no paved driving tours.

The park's remote location ensures plenty of clear nights for stargazing. McDonald Observatory, about two hours from Guadalupe, offers daytime tours as well as viewing nights, with reservations strongly suggested.

Standing in the Gap
Cumberland Gap National Historical Park

I looked for a man among them who would build up the wall and stand before me in the gap on behalf of the land so I would not have to destroy it, but I found none.

Ezekiel 22:30

The Cumberland Gap is a V-shaped notch in the Cumberland Mountains, which are part of the Appalachians, near where Kentucky, Virginia, and Tennessee meet. It was the first great gateway to the West and the only practical way through the Appalachian chain for a hundred miles to the north and south. Native Americans used the Gap long before the arrival of Europeans, who fought with the tribes to push their way through. Among those first travelers was well-known frontiersman Daniel Boone.

The French and Indian War halted further exploration of the Gap, but after the war's conclusion, hunters again roamed the area. In 1773, surveying parties began arriving. Boone, employed by a land speculation company, helped blaze a trail through the Gap and later led families across it to the West.

The trickle of settlers eventually became a torrent. Estimates are that between two hundred thousand and three hundred thousand people traveled through the Gap between 1775 and 1810, especially after the trail was widened to accommodate wagons and cattle drives. During the Civil War, Union and Confederate forces fought over control of the strategic spot. Toward the end of the century, attempts were made to mine the area's resources, but eventually the land became desolate and neglected until a highway was built through it.

The National Park Service dedicated Cumberland Gap National Historical Park on July 4, 1959. Following the completion of a tunnel for traffic, an approximation of the original pioneer route was established.

In Ezekiel 22, God warns the Israelites about the judgment that would surely come if they persisted in their sins. The chapter includes a catalog of the people's many wrongdoings—injustice, murder, theft, and profaning the Lord, among them—and the inevitable conclusion. God sought in vain for someone to stem the tide, to halt the rush of people racing toward ruin. In one of the saddest verses in Scripture, from Ezekiel 22:30, he found no one.

Nearly everything starts with just one. I know, because I'm a beneficiary of one.

On July 18, 1943, a fifty-six-year-old woman lay in a hospital in Madison, Wisconsin, knowing that cancer would soon take her life. She typed out her funeral and burial instructions, then her thoughts and expressions of love to her friends, husband, and five sons, concluding: "Please grant me [this] last request: to raise all my grandchildren Christians and early lead to the Saving knowledge of the Lord Jesus Christ."

To the wives of the oldest three boys, the fiancée of the fourth, and the future wife of the fifth, she continued, "Guide my grandchildren to Christ Jesus for Salvation, redemption and release. God has entrusted you with a sacred charge."

That woman was my grandmother, her youngest son my father. He hadn't even met my mother—that wouldn't happen for four more years—and I wasn't born for several more years. Yet I'm firmly convinced that my grandmother played a major role in my life as a Christian.

I grew up in a church-going home, but the concept of salvation—I didn't even know the term—wasn't mentioned. Then, in the summer after tenth grade, a guest speaker at our youth group boldly declared that a vague, fuzzy, feel-good kind of love for God was not enough: God wanted a personal relationship with each of us, and he sent his Son Jesus to earth to accomplish that. I immediately knew what the speaker was saying was true. I started reading the Scriptures for the first time, and began growing in grace and knowledge, a journey that continues to this day.

Several years later, my mother was cleaning out her basement and found a little wordless book from Child Evangelism Fellowship. Imagine my surprise to see my name written in my own hand on the back page, indicating that I had asked Jesus to be my Savior at age six! I vaguely remembered the neighborhood meetings, but not the decision. But the Lord had not forgotten.

What had prepared me as a young child and then as a teenager to receive salvation? I believe it was the prayers of a grandmother I never met. A grandmother who asked the Lord to reach across the generations and take hold of loved ones she would never know. She did the only thing she could do for us, which was the best.

Inspired by Grandma's final letter, I have committed to pray for my relatives, those alive now and those still to come. I'm honored to take up her mantle, the finest legacy I could ever hope to leave behind.

Will you be that one for your family? I know what you're thinking. *I'm just one person!* I put up the same argument. But you know what? God was only looking for a solitary individual to intercede on behalf of a culture heading in the wrong direction.

Like my grandmother, you might not be around to see what your prayers accomplish. That's why, if you're willing to take up the challenge, you should keep a record. Write out your thoughts and prayers so that your descendants know the story of how you stood in the gap for them.

See It for Yourself:

Cumberland Gap National Historical Park: *www.nps.gov/cuga*

This park offers cascading waterfalls, lush forests, miles of walking paths, a cave tour, and a panoramic view of the three states the park includes.

Another notable feature is in the Visitor Center, where quotations from those who trekked through the Gap hang on banners. Because most people traveled through anonymously, the words are culled from stories handed down from their ancestors. There's a form to fill out if you have a story from your own family's history.

Strangers and Aliens
Ellis Island

Do not oppress an alien; you yourselves know how it feels to be aliens, because you were aliens in Egypt.

Exodus 23:9

More than twelve million immigrants entered the United States during the years 1892 to 1954 through Ellis Island, the immigration museum that is part of the Statue of Liberty National Monument. President Lyndon Johnson signed an act to refurbish the derelict buildings in August 1965, but it wasn't open to the public until the 1980s. Who came through this immigration station? Foreigners, also called strangers and aliens.

Not too long ago, a speaker at our church challenged us to look up the words *stranger* and *alien* in the Bible. So I hauled out my big concordance, which is a book listing all the words used in Scripture and where to find them (of course, you can also use online resources and apps, but I like my hardcover).

I was surprised to discover how many references I found. In 2 Chronicles 2:17, I learned that around the time of King Solomon's reign there were over 150 thousand strangers and aliens (non-Israelites) in his country, about a tenth of its population. Many of them were unskilled workers.

I wonder if because the Israelites were God's chosen people, they tended to look down on foreigners. And whether that might be why the Lord often reminded them in the books of Exodus and Deuteronomy that they too were once ill-used and disrespected outsiders: "[God] defends the cause of the fatherless and the widow, and loves the alien, giving him food and clothing. And you are to love those who are aliens, for you yourselves were aliens in Egypt" (Deuteronomy 10:18-19). In the Gospels, Jesus reiterated this compassion for strangers by telling his followers to love God first then love their neighbor as themselves; to visit the hungry, needy, sick, and prisoners; and to interact with the lowest of society.

Did you ever think about the hardships immigrant families—perhaps yours—experienced? Did they find anyone who cared for them despite their different accents and customs, regardless of how they got here?

My mother-in-law started kindergarten in New York City knowing just Italian. The school promptly booted her out and told her to only return when she could speak English. Although she was a native-born citizen, her parents were from the old country and barely knew English, and her neighborhood consisted of all the same kind of people. Learning a new language couldn't have been easy for her.

How my heart aches for that little girl! I never asked her—and it's too late now—but I hope someone took pity on her and helped her when she finally made it back to school. Undoubtedly she still struggled to understand what her classmates and teachers said.

This is not about immigration policy. Christians can have differing opinions about what our government should do. But concerning our attitude toward the strangers and aliens among us right now, God's directive is clear—we are to love, care for, and empathize with them.

When you think about it, that shouldn't be too hard for us. Like the Israelites, we know how it feels. We also are strangers and aliens, outsiders caught between our earthly, native home, and the full citizenship we won't achieve until we reach heaven.

See for Yourself

Ellis Island: *www.nps.gov/elis*

The ferry ride to Liberty and Ellis Islands is easier from New Jersey's Liberty State Park. Parking there is stress-free and less costly, and the crowds are less than in downtown Manhattan, the other starting point for the ferry.

Airport-style security is in place for both the Statue of Liberty and Ellis Island, but don't let that deter you. Make a day of it by taking in both sites on one ferry ticket. After all, millions of Americans can trace their ancestry to the immigrants who passed through there— maybe even yours! Search ship passenger records for family names at Ellis Island, or online at *www.libertyellisfoundation.org*.

The Great Hall has been restored to appear as it did a century ago, and the exhibits chronicle life at this port of entry, telling individual stories and exploring our nation's four centuries of immigration history. Join a free, ranger-led tour for even more insights.

If you're in downtown New York, consider checking out these other free or low cost national park sites:

- Castle Clinton National Monument, which processed immigrants before Ellis Island opened, and is located near the Manhattan ferry port. (*www.nps.gov/cacl*)

- Governor's Island National Monument is a great place to walk and ride bikes while learning about military history and enjoying outstanding views of New York City; the short boat ride there is only a couple of bucks. (*www.nps.gov/gois*)

- Federal Hall National Memorial on Wall Street is the site where George Washington took his oath of office. Now it's a museum dedicated to our government's beginnings. (*www.nps.gov/feha*)

- African Burial Ground National Monument, the city's newest park site, contains artifacts related to the 1991 discovery of a seventeenth- and eighteenth-century cemetery for free and enslaved Africans. (*www.nps.gov/afbg*)

In New Jersey, visit:

- Paterson Great Falls National Historical Park is where manufacturers harnessed water to power the Industrial Revolution. (*www.nps.gov/pagr*)

Are You Assimilating—or Adapting?
Assateague Island National Seashore

*Yet, O Lord, you are our Father. We are the clay, you are the potter; we
are all the work of your hand.*

Isaiah 64:8

I've never been to a national lakeshore or seashore, much to my
regret, because I love the beach. All four of the Park Service's national
lakeshores are on the Great Lakes, while the ten national seashores
lie along the Atlantic, Gulf, and Pacific coasts. I think the one I'd like
most to visit is Assateague.

Assateague is a barrier island, shaped by both natural and human
forces. Waves, wind, and rain continually alter the sand and dry land.
People affect the water quality, and plant and animal life. One more
factor affects the island's ecology and popularity—the horses.

If you've read Marguerite Henry's "Misty of Chincoteague" series of
children's novels about the ponies, you are already familiar with their
story. Wild ponies, descendants of domesticated animals brought

in over three hundred years ago, roam the island, which is divided between Maryland and Virginia. Most of the Maryland portion makes up the national seashore, while the Virginia part is the Chincoteague National Wildlife Refuge, managed by the United States Fish & Wildlife Service. A fence at the state line separates the animals into two herds. On the last Wednesday in July, nearly all of the sixty to ninety foals born annually within the Virginia herd are auctioned to benefit the Chincoteague Volunteer Fire Department.

One of the "Misty" books, *Stormy, Misty's Foal*, takes its inspiration from the real-life Ash Wednesday nor'easter of 1962, a destructive squall that ravaged the East Coast for nearly three days. That storm took a toll on Assateague and Chincoteague Islands, their coastlines, and their horses. Many of the actual and fictitious ponies died, but in the story, Misty and her newborn, Stormy, survived.

These Assateague equines have to be hardy to endure because of the extreme weather and a food supply never intended to support these non-natives. The abundant yet nutrient-poor salt marshes lead the ponies to drink so much water they appear bloated.

Visitors enthralled by the sight of the beautiful animals running free try to feed and pet them. But people food makes them sick, and horses that learn to beg for it are in danger of being hit by cars.

Only the fittest, strongest, and smartest of these ponies survive. Their secret? Adapting to their environment.

My online dictionary says that to adapt to is to adjust or change, especially to difficult circumstances, conditions, or requirements. In my thesaurus, the word *assimilate* is used as a synonym for *adapt.* But I think a subtle distinction exists between the two words. Assimilating implies conforming, looking no different from anything or anyone else.

Christians are to be adapters, not assimilators. The apostle Paul models that in 1 Corinthians 9:19: "Though I am free and belong to no man, I make myself a slave to everyone, to win as many as possible." He goes on to explain how he adjusts to those he ministers to—Jews, Gentiles, strict Law abiders, and weak believers, all without betraying his own beliefs. "I have become all things to all men so that by all possible means I might save some. I do all this for the sake of the gospel" (vv. 22-23).

Scripture recognizes that as things around us change, so must we. Paul discovered this truth through experiences that touched him personally: "I have learned to be content whatever the circumstances. I know what it is to be in need, and I know what it is to have plenty" (Philippians 4:11-12).

Jesus remains the highest example of adapting without compromise. He left his position in heaven to become God in human form, for our benefit.

How do we follow these biblical models? Like the Assateague horses, we must be fit, strong, and smart, yet humble and willing to be shaped. We need to remain fervent but pliable in the midst of imperfect surroundings and events, through the discipline of studying Scripture, accompanied by prayer and praise. We have to acquire wisdom and know how to apply it, being "shrewd as snakes" while staying "innocent as doves," as Jesus advises in Matthew 10:16.

Finally, we're obliged to do all this while submitting to God's will for us. A tall order, for sure! His absolute sovereignty gives him the right to mold us as he desires, not capriciously, but with great love, for his pleasure and our good. We're not left alone to accomplish this by ourselves either. God assures us the battle isn't ours (1 Samuel 17:47, 2 Chronicles 20:15), nor are the burdens too heavy (Psalm 55:22, Matthew 11:28-30, 1 Peter 5:7).

Still, some days I feel as battered as a barrier island, and instead of calling on God's survival skills to adapt, I "go along to get along." I flirt with the ever-present temptation of feeding on what the world says will fill me, and end up not transformed, but conformed.

It takes a heap of humility and a lot of practice for us to yield to God's will. The experience isn't always pleasant. But the result is a wonder to behold—peace beyond understanding, and in due time, unrestrained jubilation, and freedom beyond our wildest dreams.

Kind of like the magnificent horses of Assateague.

See for Yourself

Assateague Island National Seashore: *www.nps.gov/asis*

This park's entrances are by bridge from the north in Maryland, or by a southern route through Chincoteague, Virginia. Once on the thirty-seven-mile-long island, ditch the car and hop on your own bike.

In addition to the main road, trails offer plenty of ways to explore on two wheels or on foot. Campers are welcome, but be prepared for bugs, sand, and wind. Canoe and kayak rentals are available seasonally, with fishing, clamming, swimming, ranger-led wildlife tours, and birding among other popular activities. Best to bring your own food and water—there are public fountains in a few locations, with bottled water available during summer. Virginia has even less options. Restaurants are off-island.

You can bring your own horse—and reserve a camping spot for it! Visitors may ride on a limited area of the beach on the Maryland side from early October through mid-May, weather permitting, and in Virginia year-round within a similarly restricted zone.

Fire!
Yellowstone National Park

Fear not, for I have redeemed you; I have summoned you by name;
you are mine. When you pass through the waters, I will be with you;
and when you pass through the rivers, they will not sweep over you.
When you walk through the fire, you will not be burned; the flames
will not set you ablaze. For I am the Lord, your God, the Holy One of
Israel, your Savior.

Isaiah 43:1-3

During a visit to Yellowstone National Park, I read about the spectacular fire that occurred in 1988. That summer was the driest in the park's recorded history, and by mid-July, about six thousand acres had burned. After little more than a week, flames flared over twice that amount, and by the end of the month, drought and high winds created an almost unmanageable inferno.

Firefighters around the country arrived to help in what became the nation's largest fire-fighting effort. The story made national news. On the worst day, in August, gusts pushed the fire across more than 150 acres. The first snows in September helped dampen the blaze, and the immediate threat to life and property was over, but the last of the fire wasn't extinguished until November.

We tend to think of forest fires as bad, and yet good comes from naturally occurring fires. The Yellowstone blazes affected 36 percent of the park's acreage, but those lands weren't devastated. Fires stimulate the regrowth of trees and bushes, and clear away undergrowth to make way for new development. Though grass and shrubs are consumed, their belowground root systems usually aren't harmed. In fact, more sunlight and the enriching ash left behind increases their productivity for a few years afterward.

The lodgepole pines, which make up 80 percent of Yellowstone's canopy, depend on fires for propagation. The intense heat opens their resin-sealed cones, releasing the seeds to spread and make more trees.

Fire is a given in life, the physical as well as the emotional and spiritual kinds. To avoid physical fires, we do everything we can to prevent them—inspecting our homes' wiring, installing smoke detectors, purchasing flameproof sleepwear, teaching our kids not to play with matches, etc. Healthy relationships with others and a close and continual walk with the Lord through prayer and Bible reading help keep emotional and spiritual flares at bay.

But sometimes fire comes, no matter what we do. I love the very honest Old Testament account of Shadrach, Meshach, and Abednego, found in Daniel 3. Babylonian King Nebuchadnezzar, essentially their captor, threatened to toss the trio into a raging furnace because they wouldn't bow down and worship his statue: "Then what god will be able to rescue you from my hand?" (v. 15), he taunted. But they stood their ground: "We do not need to defend ourselves before you in this matter. If we are thrown into the blazing furnace, the God we serve is able to save us from it, and he will rescue us from your hand. But even if he does not, we want you to know that we will not serve your gods or worship the image of gold you have set up" (vv. 16-18).

What amazing faith! Faced with a torturous death, they refused to renounce God and trusted him to either save them or help them die.

Perhaps you know the result of that confrontation, how a furious Nebuchadnezzar ordered the fire heated seven times hotter, tied up the three "rebels," and had them thrown in. The heat was so blistering the soldiers who did the deed perished.

As he peered into the inferno, Nebuchadnezzar got the shock of his life. "Weren't there three men that we tied up and threw into the fire?" he asked his advisors. He was astounded to see a fourth man walking around in the fire, unbound and unharmed, who "looks like a son of the gods" (vv. 24-25).

Bible scholars and commentators speculate that what Nebuchadnezzar saw in the flames may have been an angel or possibly a pre-incarnate appearance of Jesus. At any rate, the king quickly realized that whoever this other being was, he was indeed mightier than Nebuchadnezzar's gods, who could never have saved the men. Shadrach, Meshach, and Abednego emerged from that furnace so unscathed that in addition to not being injured, they didn't even smell like smoke!

Scripture is clear in affirming that everyone, Christian or not, will go through fires in this life. Job, that biblical epitome of suffering, ruefully noted, "Man is born to trouble as surely as sparks fly upward" (Job 5:7), and Jesus bluntly states in John 16:33, "In this world you will have trouble." He follows it up with this assurance: "But take heart! I have overcome the world."

I've passed through many fires of varying intensity, and I realize future ones are in store. No doubt you can relate. But there is someone willing to go through the flames with us, the God who asks us to give him all our heart, soul, mind, and strength. He backs up his demand with tender and compassionate promises, such as this: "In this you greatly rejoice, though now for a little while you may have had to suffer grief in all kinds of trials. These have come so that your faith— of greater worth than gold, which perishes even though refined by fire—may be proved genuine and may result in praise, glory and honor when Jesus Christ is revealed" (1 Peter 1:6-7).

It isn't just the lodgepole pine that God designed to flourish under fire.

See for Yourself

Yellowstone National Park: *www.nps.gov/yell*

This park, straddling parts of Idaho, Montana, and Wyoming, sits on top of an active volcano and one of the world's largest calderas—areas formed by the collapse of land following an eruption. While it has about one thousand to three thousand earthquakes annually, a result of the large number of faults associated with the volcano, sightseers need not worry. Most quakes aren't felt, and geologists say a massive eruption is unlikely to occur for at least a thousand years.

The tremors serve to maintain the hydrothermal activity the park is best known for. Yellowstone has more geothermal features than anywhere else on earth, with over three hundred geysers (such as Old

Faithful) and ten thousand other thermal features. The Norris Geyser Basin is an especially captivating area, with a boardwalk that winds through geysers, hot springs, fumaroles (steam vents), and bubbling mud pots.

It was at Yellowstone that a Princeton Seminary student and seasonal bellhop first lit a fire for God in the parks. Warren Ost went on to found A Christian Ministry in the National Parks, an organization now reaching over thirty thousand people with the gospel in thirty national parks.

Beauty is in the Eye of the God-Holder
John Muir

One thing I ask of the Lord, this is what I seek; that I may dwell in the house of the Lord all the days of my life, to gaze upon the beauty of the Lord and to seek him in his temple.

Psalm 27:4

Happy Birthday, National Park Service!

August 25 is the anniversary of the Park Service's founding in 1916. And one of the people we have to thank for this occasion is an immigrant named John Muir.

Born in Scotland in 1838, Muir and his family moved to Wisconsin eleven years later, where he learned to love nature by roaming the countryside. He spent three years at the University of Wisconsin in Madison before leaving to explore the United States and Canada, supporting himself with odd jobs along the way.

One of those jobs changed his life. Muir suffered a blinding eye injury while working at a carriage parts shop in Indianapolis, and after regaining his sight a month later, he resolved to devote himself to the outdoors. He walked from Indiana to the Gulf of Mexico, sailed to Cuba and Panama, crossed the isthmus, and continued up the West Coast, finally arriving in San Francisco in March 1868. From there he walked into the Sierra Nevada Mountains, feeling as if he'd found the loveliest place on earth.

Eventually, Muir settled down in Martinez, California, married, had two daughters, and managed his family's fruit ranch. But his wanderlust wouldn't allow him to stay in one place very long. He traveled to Alaska several times, to Europe, Australia, South America, and again and again to the Sierras.

Muir took up writing about his journeys. A series of articles for *Century* magazine decried the devastation he saw taking place at the hands of sheepherders and ranchers, especially in Yosemite Valley. Muir's words spurred Congress to create Yosemite National Park in 1890. His efforts also led to the establishment of Sequoia, Mount Rainier, Petrified Forest, and Grand Canyon National Parks. Muir co-founded the environmental group, The Sierra Club, in 1892.

Muir's 1901 book, *Our National Parks*, caught the attention of President Theodore Roosevelt, another nature enthusiast. Muir took the president on a tour of Yosemite, where the pair hatched a broad conservation plan. Roosevelt eventually set aside 148 million acres of land for national forests, five national parks, and twenty-three national monuments during his terms in office.

Little wonder that John Muir is often referred to as the "Father of the National Park Service."

The Sierra Club Bulletin's January 1916 issue was dedicated solely to Muir, memorializing his death thirteen months earlier. In it, Robert Underwood Johnson wrote, "To some, beauty seems but an accident of creation: to Muir it was the very smile of God." He related a story about his friend:

> An instance of this is told of him as he stood with an acquaintance at one of the great view-points of the Yosemite Valley and, filled with wonder and devotion, wept. His companion, more stolid than most, could not understand his feeling, and was so thoughtless as to say so.
>
> "Mon," said Muir, with the Scotch dialect into which he often lapsed, "Can ye see unmoved the glory of the Almighty?"
>
> "Oh, it's very fine," was the reply, "but I do not wear my heart upon my sleeve."
>
> "Ah, my dear mon," said Muir, "in the face of such a scene as this, it's no time to be thinkin' o' where to wear your heart."

John Muir treasured the mountains and valleys he roamed, and was convinced that others should have the opportunity to experience them in all their pristine, God-created exquisiteness. You and I are the recipients of his foresight and profound sense of wonder.

One day those who have taken Jesus as their Savior will see a far greater splendor, hard as it is for us mere mortals to envision. As the book of Revelation describes it, we will wake up to the New Jerusalem, shining with God's glory, brilliant as a precious jewel, with walls of gorgeously colored gems, pearl gates, streets of gold, and a crystal-clear river. "Your eyes will see the king in his beauty," Isaiah prophesied (Isaiah 33:17).

I imagine I'd weep at the sight of such loveliness, just like John Muir, except that the Bible says there's no crying in heaven.

Or perhaps when it says that God will wipe away our tears, the Bible means that he will personally dry our eyes as they well up at the breathtaking sight, and we won't give a passing thought to the heart we unashamedly wear on our sleeve.

See for Yourself

John Muir's name is found throughout the Park Service, but specifically in connection with these places:

Muir Woods National Monument: *www.nps.gov/muwo*

In 1908, northern California businessman William Kent donated this uncut stand of redwoods to the federal government, and Theodore Roosevelt designated it as a national monument. Kent asked that it be named after Muir, and the president obliged. Said Muir, "This is the best tree-lover's monument that could possibly be found in all the forests of the world. You have done me great honor, and I am proud of it."

Today visitors can still hike among the quiet, magnificent groves, located eleven miles north of the Golden Gate Bridge. Parking is limited, so use the Marin County shuttle instead. The bus operates seasonally on weekends and during winter holidays.

The John Muir Trail: *www.pcta.org/discover-the-trail/john-muir-trail*

This rugged 211-mile track runs from Yosemite Valley to Mt. Whitney in California, mostly in conjunction with the Pacific Crest Trail Association. The route winds through Yosemite, Sequoia, and Kings Canyon National Parks, with elevations reaching up to fourteen thousand feet.

John Muir National Historic Site: *www.nps.gov/jomu*

The Muir home is about thirty miles east of San Francisco in the Alhambra Valley. Ranger or docent-led tours of the house's first floor are scheduled daily, with additional ones on the weekends. Take a cell phone tour to explore the nine-acre grounds on your own. The orchard produces many different types of fruit, and visitors may pick and take home small amounts.

P.S. Here is the Park Service's birthday gift to *you*—free admission to all parks every August 25!

Fall

Autumn's On Its Way
Rocky Mountain National Park

For the Lord himself will come down from heaven, with a loud command, with the voice of the archangel and with the trumpet call of God.

1 Thessalonians 4:16

Fall is a special time in Colorado's Rocky Mountain National Park. The aspens flare into brilliant red and gold, and the elk bugle.

Huh? The animals put on a concert?

Well, sort of. During the summer, these members of the deer family tend to hang out in the park's higher tundra elevation seeking food, then move down the mountains as the weather turns cooler to feed among the meadows' tall grasses and shrubs. They also come to breed.

Weighing over a thousand pounds and crowned with impressively large antlers, the males scope out the females, knowing the competition is fierce. They do a lot of preening, helped along by a splash of "cologne," which in the elk's case is a strong musky odor. Then they let loose with their "come hither" voice.

The bull elk signal, or bugle, is a swelling of deep, resonant tones, which builds to a high-pitched squeal then drops to a succession of grunts. The peculiar noise serves to attract cow elk, to intimidate rivals, and possibly to release tension. The distinct sound generally is heard around dawn and then again at dusk.

Visitors may spot elk elsewhere in the park the rest of the year, but in the fall, they usually gather in Kawuneeche Valley, Horseshoe Park, Moraine Park, and Upper Beaver Meadows. They also amble into the park gateway town of Estes Park, where the residents love them so much that they hold an annual Elk Fest in their honor. This free festival is held the first weekend in October. During the fest, you can compete in the Elk Bugling Contest, using either a horn or your own vocal cords.

One chilly autumn Sunday morning when I was in college, my roommate and I left our apartment for the short walk to church. We were surprised to find we were the only ones there. Puzzled, we searched the sanctuary and all the other rooms, and found not a soul. Eventually it dawned on us that we had forgotten to "fall back," to turn our clocks back an hour, so we had arrived before anyone else (for a change). Paula breathed a sigh of relief. "I thought the Rapture had occurred and we weren't taken!"

We still laugh about our twenty-year-old selves back then, young Christians who had an incomplete understanding of what Jesus's second coming looked like. All we knew was that we didn't want to miss it.

We won't. Neither will anyone else who is alive at the time. Scripture is clear about that.

Jesus's next and last appearance will be accompanied by occurrences the world over—a darkened sun and moon, falling stars, and Jesus visibly shining gloriously in the sky (Matthew 24:27-30).

Even before we see these spectacles, our attention will be captured with a shout and the unique, definitive sound of . . . *a bugle* (Matthew 24:31, 1 Thessalonians 4:16). Those resonances will be even more distinctive and unmistakable than an elk in autumn, one that will leave no doubt in anyone's mind as to its origin.

Hard to wrap your mind around such an event, isn't it? That's why the topic of when and where it will happen is of such endless fascination, conjecture, and even anxiety. The Bible warns that there will be people who take advantage of our curiosity and uncertainty by saying they have all the answers, or even claiming they are Jesus, bugling for all their worth in an attempt to mimic the real deal.

In light of this, Peter asks his readers, "What kind of people ought you to be? You ought to live holy and godly lives as you look forward to the day of God and speed its coming" (2 Peter 3:11-12).

His instruction is still relevant today. What does that waiting, watching, and working look like? Jesus tells us in the parable of the ten virgins in Matthew 25, where he describes wedding guests anticipating the groom's arrival to start the festivities. They fell asleep in the meantime, but the minute they heard the groom's shout, the ones who'd planned and brought enough oil to keep their lamps lit were ready to go. Faithful servants may get tired while waiting, yet they keep doing whatever their master has given them to do until he comes back to relieve them.

For those who follow Christ, there is no fear of missing the bugle, only eager expectation and a shared hope in that bright day of celebration. A day when pain and evil are gone forever, and death, the final enemy, is conquered.

Are you ready for the bugle? Lift up your head—autumn's on its way!

See for Yourself

Rocky Mountain National Park: *www.nps.gov/romo*

The park is open year-round, although some areas may be closed depending on weather conditions. The scenic Trail Ridge Road, the park's fifty-mile main thoroughfare, featuring plenty of trails and picturesque overlooks, climbs to 12,183 feet above sea level.

There are five campgrounds, and reservations are strongly suggested during the busy summer and fall months. While there is no other lodging within the park, Estes Park at the eastern entrance and Grand Lake on the west have plenty of options. Good news for Y members: the YMCA of the Rockies in Estes Park offers a discount for its rooms, cabins, and vacation homes.

Keep a safe distance between you and the elk, as you should with any wildlife. They've been known to ram cars, especially during the mating season. And leave the wildflowers where they are for others to enjoy. (On a personal note: I'm speaking to you, Amy!)

Holding Out for a Hero
Flight 93 National Memorial

And what more shall I say? I do not have time to tell about Gideon, Barak, Samson, Jephthah, David, Samuel and the prophets, who through faith conquered kingdoms, administered justice, and gained what was promised; who shut the mouths of lions, quenched the fury of the flames, and escaped the edge of the sword; whose weakness was turned to strength; and who became powerful in battle and routed foreign armies...Some faced jeers and flogging, while still others were chained and put in prison. They were stoned; they were sawed in two; they were put to death by the sword. They went about in sheepskins and goatskins, destitute, persecuted and mistreated.

Hebrews 11:32-34, 36-37

Hard to believe it's been so many years since the 9/11 attacks.

Many communities and national parks organize observances on the anniversary of 9/11. Special observances are held at the Pentagon and in Manhattan, where three of the four commercial airliners were deliberately crashed on that fateful day in 2001. The Park Service also holds a solemn remembrance at the Flight 93 National Memorial in Shanksville, Pennsylvania, the spot where forty passengers and crew thwarted an assault on the Capitol at the expense of their own lives. This memorial is the only National Park Service site wholly dedicated to telling the story of the terrorist attacks.

Speeches about the victims' bravery usually are included in the ceremonies. They're called heroes, and rightly so.

When I think of heroes, I'm reminded of the "Hall of Faith" in Hebrews 11. The list is impressive; some names and accounts are well known, others less so. An interesting exercise is to look up and read in the Old Testament about each of the people and/or episodes cited in the entire chapter. Laudable exploits aren't all you'll find, though. You'll also discover individuals with notable flaws.

Take Jephthah, for instance. What we know about him comes from just two chapters, Judges 11 and 12. We learn he was born in Gilead, a mountainous region east of the Jordan inhabited by the tribes of Gad, Reuben, and the southern part of Manasseh. The text is hazy about who his father was, but not about his mother: she was a prostitute. Jephthah is described as a mighty warrior, but his disreputable background meant he had no rights of inheritance. His legitimate half-brothers kicked him out of the house, and Jephthah subsequently took up with a band of thugs and became their chief.

Soon enough, though, the village elders came looking for him, not to punish him further, but to enlist his help as commander to fight off their enemies. "Didn't you hate me and drive me from my father's house?" Jephthah asked them. "Suppose you take me back to fight the Ammonites and the Lord gives them to me—will I really be your head?" (Judges 11:7, 9). They assured him he would.

The former outsider became the ultimate insider, with enough authority to exact his revenge. Yet he did not. He first sought a diplomatic solution with the Ammonites, confident in the knowledge that the land they claimed was theirs did in fact belong to Israel.

When that didn't work, Jephthah went to battle, filled with the Spirit of the Lord, and won.

But in the heat of the moment, Jephthah made a rash and disastrous vow. He pledged that if God gave him the victory, he'd sacrifice whatever came out of his house to meet him when he returned in triumph. Regrettably, that turned out to be his only child.

Heroes are often made of ordinary people doing extraordinary things in unusual circumstances. The passengers and crew going about their regular business on United Flight 93 had no idea they would be called to heroics that day. Jephthah undoubtedly figured he'd carry the stigma of rejection all his life and never get a chance to redeem himself. His daughter didn't know that her death, made willingly to not disgrace the Lord or her father, would be annually commemorated by the young women of Israel.

Followers of Jesus can be sure that a life of faith makes such deeds of courage, might, and perseverance possible, not just for prominent believers, but also for the average Joe and Jane Pewsitter. The writer of Hebrews lists names at first in chapter eleven. Then he seems to realize it's impossible to include all who acted bravely, righteously, and miraculously, despite their weaknesses. The common thread is that their faith in a powerful God made them strong when they needed to be.

Most of us won't ever be jailed, sawed in half, or stoned for our beliefs. If you're like me, when you hear of things like this happening to Christians in other parts of the world, you pray for them and perhaps wonder how you'd react in the same circumstances—then pray again that you'll never find out. Scripture is clear that we should be prepared for negative consequences for living for Christ—mocking, ill-treatment, and affliction, at the very least.

Serving the Lord calls for endurance. Whatever acts of valor, courage, or perseverance we perform for him, large or small, known or in secret, let's determine to press on. What awaits us is a fabulous heroes' welcome from the lips of the Hero of Heroes himself:

"Well done, good and faithful servant!"

See for Yourself

Flight 93 National Memorial: *www.nps.gov/flni*

The memorial is an open field, meaning there's very little shade, so fall is a good time to visit. At the Visitor Center Complex, you'll find exhibits and the Flight Path Walkway and Overlook. Interpretive panels and the Wall of Names are at the Memorial Plaza crash site. Free cell phone tours are available to further enhance your visit.

For those unable to travel to the memorial, the park website offers virtual tours, interactive elements, and many more features.

Waiting on Hope
Carlsbad Caverns National Park

We rejoice in hope of the glory of God. Not only so, but we also rejoice in our sufferings, because we know that suffering produces perseverance; perseverance, character; and character, hope. And hope does not disappoint us, because God has poured out his love into our hearts by the Holy Spirit, whom he has given us.

Romans 5:2-5

Caves hold a special fascination for me. There's just something so cool—literally and figuratively—about descending beneath the earth and discovering a new world, one that is dim, eerie, and miraculously filled with astounding shapes and cavities. So naturally, when my family and I were in New Mexico, we stopped at Carlsbad Caverns.

How Carlsbad evolved from a guano (bird and bat droppings) mining area to a renowned geological site is part of American Southwest history. Native Americans were the first inhabitants living within the park boundaries, and some of their cooking ring sites and pictographs still exist there. Spanish explorers came next, claiming the region for their country, until Mexico took over—then lost it to the United States. The first person to find the caverns' entrance is disputed, but it may have been a sixteen-year-old cowhand in 1898.

Photographs of the interior appeared around 1915, landing in the *New York Times* in 1923. Those pictures, along with surveys and maps, lead to the recommendation that Carlsbad become a national monument, which happened in October of that year. It achieved national park status seven years later.

Aside from walking through the twisting cave, another attraction at Carlsbad is the nightly bat show. Brazilian free-tailed bats sail out of the caverns in a mass exodus at dusk, and apparently, it's a captivating sight. My husband was very excited to see it, but our daughter wasn't. She was at that age where everything her parents wanted to do was automatically labeled boring. So I volunteered to stay with her at our hotel, and my mother, who'd come along with us on the trip, went with my husband to observe the bats.

As I heard the story later, the two of them settled into their seats in the park's amphitheater in the fading early evening light, surprised to discover they were the only ones there. A ranger gave a short talk on the nocturnal creatures, and then the three of them waited for the bats to make their appearance.

And waited. And waited. Not a single bat flew out of the cave the entire time. The ranger shrugged and said it happened sometimes. They all finally gave up and left.

Hope. It can be as minor as looking for bats, or as gut wrenching as holding your breath for a doctor's diagnosis. My husband was ticked off that he didn't get what he expected, while Mom was more philosophical, but they both got over it.

Major heartaches and disappointments aren't as easily dismissed. Old wounds and unfulfilled desires, buried deep in the heart, awaken at the slightest touch.

Like me, you undoubtedly have your own frustrations, regrets, and dashed dreams. Cynicism and disillusionment may nip uncomfortably close to your heels. World and national news stir up nothing but pessimism. Some days it's difficult to feel hopeful about this old world and very easy to join the chorus of complainers or wallow in self-pity.

The thing is, hope that's focused on anything or anyone but God will always disappoint in the end. Circumstances and people change: we're up one minute and down the next, bats appear or maybe they don't. God remains constant. Life is that simple—and that hard.

Caves form over time by the never-ending drip, drip, drip of water on rock. But oh, what magnificence comes out of this slow but steady process! How much more beauty results when we let the poured-out love of God flow over our disenchanted hearts!

Invite God into the process. Ask him to help you look beyond the pain and pangs of your hurts to the riches he offers—perseverance, character, and above all, glorious hope.

See for Yourself

Carlsbad Caverns National Park: *www.nps.gov/cave*

Actor and comedian Will Rogers called Carlsbad "the Grand Canyon with a roof over it," and you'll understand why once you see the spectacular limestone formations within the huge space. You won't have to descend in a guano bucket or rope ladder like those initial pioneers, though. There's an elevator, or if you prefer, take the steep, winding walkway to the natural entrance. There are two self-guided hikes along (mostly) paved pathways (rent audio guides for a fuller experience), or several ranger-guided tours for additional fees—for most of those, you'll need batteries for lights, as well as helmets, gloves, and knee and elbow pads supplied by the park.

Here's a bit of trivia for you film buffs: The 1959 movie *Journey to the Center of the Earth* was shot in portions of Carlsbad.

Oh, and those bats? They usually fly out from Memorial Day weekend through October—*if* they decide to show up...

It's All in Your Head
Homestead National Monument

Your attitude should be the same as that of Christ Jesus: Who, being in very nature God, did not consider equality with God something to be grasped, but made himself nothing, taking the very nature of a servant, being made in human likeness. And being found in appearance as a man, he humbled himself and became obedient to death—even death on a cross! Therefore God exalted him to the highest place and gave him the name that is above every name, that at the name of Jesus every knee should bow, in heaven and on earth and under the earth, and every tongue confess that Jesus Christ is Lord, to the glory of God the Father.

Philippians 2:5-11

I learned how to make candles when I was at Homestead National Monument.

Let me back up a bit. Several years ago, as an Artist in Residence at Homestead, I spent three weeks in the place the National Park Service sets aside to commemorate the Homestead Act of 1862.

You *do* remember this important piece of legislation from American history class, right? Hmmm…just as I thought. You vaguely recall mention of it, but after taking the test you promptly forgot all the salient points.

Me too. I had some serious studying to do before I went.

The Homestead Act, crafted during the Civil War, guaranteed 160 acres of land free to anyone who was a citizen or planned to become one. A homesteader had to be at least twenty-one years old and the head of a household, and had five years to "prove up" the claim, that is, to plant crops and build a house, before the land became his or hers. Ten percent of the United States—270 million acres of public land—was claimed and settled by private citizens under the Act. Congress repealed the law in 1976, with a ten-year extension for the state of Alaska.

For my residency, I wrote and performed a one-woman show based on my research. *Steal Away: The Story of a Homesteader and an Exoduster* is about former slaves who fled the South after Reconstruction ended. I portrayed a homesteader who meets and tells the story of a family of Exodusters, so named because they likened their flight to the exodus of the Israelites out of Egypt.

So there I was at Homestead, all settled in to write and later perform my play. But the park rangers were scrambling in preparation for the deluge of kids expected during the annual September Pioneer Days event, and they requested my help in making candles.

I called upon my Girl Scout skills and built a fire. It only took me an hour and a half—hey, those scouting days were a long time ago! Then I melted beeswax and beef tallow together, cut string for the wicks, and began to dip, dip, dip.

Do you know how many layers it takes to make a decent sized candle? Waaay too many. But I persevered and cranked out 120 of those babies.

Candle making is a painstaking and messy job. It's hot. Smoke stings your eyes. Wax drips all over you. My shoulders and back stiffened up as I leaned over the huge iron kettle. To top it off, I wore an ankle-length outfit—dressed up as a long-ago homesteader, naturally—and constantly worried I'd set myself on fire.

Let's just say that over the course of the day I developed a fervent appreciation for these modern times when I can buy candles in a store. Making them the old-fashioned way, I concluded, is highly overrated.

Here are some other lovely thoughts that coursed through my head as I coaxed tiny sparks to take hold, then plunged string after string into the pot: *I came here to write, not do grunt work! This is a real waste of my talent. I bet other artists in residence in other parks don't spend their days like this!* And on and on.

The truth is that I had plenty of time for writing and a whole lot more at Homestead. I enjoyed the Traditions Festival presentations of singing and dancing from a variety of cultures, helped with a poetry workshop for high schoolers, rehearsed and performed my show, took long walks through the prairie, and drank in the wide-open Plains sky.

Pioneer Days is a big event, requiring all hands on deck and many volunteers to make it a success. And my candle making freed up a ranger to do other necessary work. I could have said no when I was first asked to help with the candles, but that wouldn't have been the homesteading spirit, now would it?

Nor would it have been of the Holy Spirit, I realized again when I flipped open my Bible to Philippians 2 later. "Each of you should look

not only to your own interests, but also to the interests of others."
Gulp.

That was Friday. And there were still more candles to make on Saturday. When I was asked to handle that task again, I said (cue the inward sigh) yes.

Guess what? God graciously took my still-reluctant obedience and turned it around. Saturday evening my housemate, who was the same age as my daughter, invited me to accompany her and a young ranger to church and then out for ice cream. I enjoyed getting to know these two Christians who didn't mind hanging out with someone old enough to be their mother.

Because I'd had so much fun, when my roomie announced she planned to spend time making candles on Sunday, *I actually offered to join her!* The work went quickly with two pairs of hands. We chatted away as we filled our quota, and had such a great fire that we celebrated with a weenie roast and s'mores!

I became very good at making candles that fall in Nebraska. I must admit, though, I'd just as soon never use that particular skill again. Yet boring, tedious tasks are part of everyday life. I may not be dipping wicks in wax these days, but I have plenty of other chores on my list that I approach with great reluctance.

How about you? You too must have some trying and seemingly thankless assignments the Lord's plopped in your lap.

Go ahead—ask him to change the circumstances. Nothing wrong with that. God sympathizes with our weaknesses, and invites us to bring everything to him in prayer.

Just know that he often works to change *us* first, not our situations. His transformation works from the inside out. Because, as Jesus showed us, that's where real overcoming begins.

See for Yourself

Homestead National Monument: *www.nps.gov/home*

Homestead is located in Beatrice, Nebraska, on the site where the first homesteader staked his claim on January 1, 1863, the day the Act went into effect. The Heritage Center's plow shape pays homage to the fields tilled by those brave pioneers. It also looks like the bow of a ship, a reminder of the "prairie schooners" which brought people to the unsettled lands. Inside is a museum dedicated to telling the homesteading story. Beyond the center is a restored tallgrass prairie and an 1867 cabin reminiscent of early homesteader dwellings.

Over two million individual homestead claims were made over 123 years, and the estimated thirty million pieces of paper they generated are stored in the National Archives. Homestead is on a mission to digitize them. If your ancestors were homesteaders, you may be able to find their records!

Have a Fling!
Sequoia and Kings Canyon National Park

See how the farmer waits for the land to yield its valuable crop and how patient he is for the autumn and spring rains. You too, be patient and stand firm.

James 5:7-8

If you want to feel very, very small, take a trip to California's Sequoia and Kings Canyon National Parks. That's where you'll find some seventy-five groves of earth's largest living thing, the giant sequoia.

Sequoia National Park, established to protect the trees from logging, became a national park in the fall of 1890. A week later, the adjacent General Grant National Park was created and Sequoia enlarged. United States Army Cavalry troops protected both places, along with nearby Yosemite, in the early years. Congress and President Franklin D. Roosevelt created a new park, Kings Canyon, which incorporated General Grant National Park into it, and since World War II, the 1,353 square miles of both Sequoia and Kings Canyon have been administered jointly.

Just how remarkable are these huge coniferous redwoods? In the Giant Forest, so named by conservationist John Muir, stands the 275-foot tall General Sherman, the largest tree in the world by volume. Its trunk weighs an estimated 1,385 tons, its ground circumference is almost 103 feet, and its biggest branch is around seven feet in diameter. To put these largest trees' size in perspective, they are about as high as a twenty-six-story building and as wide as a city street.

That's not all. Experts believe General Sherman and other giants are between twenty-three and twenty-seven hundred years old. In 1912, logger and future parks Chief Ranger Walter Fry and five men spent several days cutting down a single sequoia. Counting the tree's growth rings, Fry was shocked to realize he'd just ended 3,266 years of growth.

What's also interesting about these behemoths is that in contrast to their great mass, their seeds are so miniscule they look like flakes. A mature tree may produce around two thousand chicken egg-sized cones a year, each bearing nearly half a million seeds.

Jesus often used natural elements like trees and seeds to illustrate spiritual truths. A prime example is the story of the sower, found in the New Testament books of Matthew, Mark, and Luke. In this parable, a farmer's seeds fall on four kinds of terrain—the hard path that ran through his field, rocky earth covered with only a thin layer of dirt, ground infested with thorns, and fertile soil. Birds quickly snatched up the first ones because the bits were just lying on the surface, unable to penetrate the packed clay. The next batch sprouted right away, but the hot sun and lack of strong root ensured the vegetation shriveled quickly. Nettles choked out the third lot, but the last group—what a harvest!

Of course, as Jesus clarified, he wasn't talking about seeds and soil, but about his message and its effect on four types of hearers: those with no understanding, emotional reactors who quickly fall away when trouble arises, people too preoccupied with life's worries to pay attention, and fruitful responders.

When I first read this parable, I zeroed in on the amount of squandered seed. Three-quarters of it never achieved permanent results! Very little gain for the investment of time and money.

Then I read a statistic that made me reconsider. In an interview with journalist David Frost, evangelist Billy Graham said he believed only about 25 percent of those who came forward at his crusades actually became Christians. Same outcome as the biblical planter!

I realized then that the way God the Sower operates is far beyond my puny human understanding. He creates up to a billion seeds in just one sequoia knowing most won't sprout, and lavishly showers his words across the world while recognizing the vast majority will fall on deaf or ultimately unresponsive ears. I tend to concentrate on what doesn't happen, while he focuses on the big picture. "As the rain and the snow come down from heaven, and do not return to it without watering the earth and making it bud and flourish, so that it yields seed for the sower and bread for the eater, so is my word that goes out from my mouth: It will not return to me empty, but will accomplish what I desire and achieve the purpose for which I sent it" (Isaiah 55:10-11).

Sequoia seeds that do take hold in the soil develop gradually over years, largely overlooked in the forest until they achieve significant height. God's work too is often slow and unobserved, done in his own way and in his own time. It sprouts from the labor of his people sent out to extravagantly sow along life's road, dispersing his message of love and forgiveness to whoever crosses their path, even among the antagonistic, superficial, and distracted. We may never know what will come from the outlay of our resources and efforts; as farmers understand, the ultimate results are out of our hands. But sow we must, because the Lord of the Harvest sets the example and calls us to carry on the task.

So fling out those seeds, no matter how little budding you see. Prepared hearts are waiting to receive them, and the reward is more glorious than even the most majestic sequoia. In God's eyes, not even one seed is wasted.

See for Yourself

Sequoia and Kings Canyon National Parks: *www.nps.gov/seki*

September 26 is National Public Lands Day, and these and other National Park Service sites are free every year on this date.

The General Highway connects Sequoia and Kings Canyon, and while driving along this loop road, be sure to stop and walk the short paths set among the giants. Many trails are paved, and guests may borrow wheelchairs at the Kings Canyon and Lodgepole Visitor Centers, and at the Giant Forest Museum.

Moro Rock is a granite dome with a steep one-quarter mile staircase to the summit, which offers stunning views. An easy 3.4-mile round-trip walk takes you to the granite cliffs and twelve hundred-foot high Tokopah Falls.

Four lodges are available for overnight stays: in Sequoia, the Wuksachi Lodge and its restaurant are open all year; so are the stone-and-timber John Muir Lodge and Grant Grove Cabins in Kings Canyon. The remote Cedar Grove Lodge in Kings Canyon operates May through mid-October. Concessions are limited between mid-October and late May. Campgrounds are numerous, with three available during winter.

Cross another park off your list while you're in the area: Yosemite is about two-and-a-half hours north of Kings Canyon.

The Sound of Silence
Haleakala National Park

The Lord is in His holy temple; let all the earth be silent before him.
Habakkuk 2:20

Do you ever think about what a park sounds like? The Park Service certainly does. Its Natural Sounds Program concerns itself with the parks' acoustic environments, the interplay of the innate physical sound sources within an area—from animals, water, and wind, for example—and the noise created by visitors. Measuring and mitigating intrusive sound levels in each of its more than four hundred units is an ongoing mission.

Sound waves are rated by their frequency and amplitude, or force, measured in decibels (dB) of sound pressure. The lower threshold of human hearing is 0 dB; a regular speaking voice registers around 65 dB. Sounds above 85dB can cause damage to our ears.

The Natural Sounds Program reports a sound level of 10 dB in Haleakala National Park's volcano crater. That's low.

My family and I can attest to that assessment. My husband and I celebrated a significant wedding anniversary with a trip to Hawaii a few years back. We chose to travel in the fall so our daughter, whose job is busiest in the summer, could join us (real romantic, right?).

Haleakala means "House of the Sun" in the Hawaiian language, and many people rise very early to ascend its 10,023-foot summit to catch the sunrise, something Mark Twain called "the sublimest spectacle I ever witnessed." However, two of us are not morning people, so we prevailed upon the third to go up in late afternoon, figuring sunset probably put on a good show as well.

We weren't disappointed. The sinking sun threw shadows throughout the crater as we looked down, watching them grow and change as the day ended. On the other side, fantastic rays, at first fiery and then more muted, shot out over the Pacific Ocean.

Aside from the gorgeous views, what we noticed most was something else Mark Twain mentioned: the silence. "Healing solitudes" was his description. He and his companions didn't say much as they stood high up, and neither did our family. "There was little conversation, for the impressive scene overawed speech," Twain wrote. "I think the memory of it will remain with me always" (Twain, 1904, 315-6).

As I stood on the summit, the majesty and power of God in the awesome, quiet space filled me. I think we three could have stood there forever drinking in the spectacular sights, except we realized it might be hard to pick our way back along the path to our car in the dark if we waited too long.

We all require peace and quiet, a soothing respite from this noisy world. As I already knew and learned again, attaining a place and time to restore body and soul isn't always easy, and tranquility can be as fleeting as a sunset. We need a way to latch on to those "healing solitudes" we crave, in the midst of our daily chaos. The God I experienced so fully on Haleakala promises that:

> Come to me, all you who are weary and burdened, and I will give you rest. Take my yoke upon you and learn from me, for I am gentle and humble in heart, and you will find rest for your souls. (Matthew 11:28-29)

> Be still, and know that I am God. (Psalm 46:10)

> Peace I leave with you; my peace I give you. I do not give to you as the world gives. Do not let your hearts be troubled and do not be afraid. (John 14:27)

Lasting serenity isn't found in a location, but in a Person. I'm glad the Park Service works to preserve special spots of stillness we can all enjoy on our travels. I'm even happier that I can reach a peace beyond comprehension wherever I am. A peace accessible to all, provided just for the asking, by the Prince of Peace himself.

He lives not only in Haleakala, but right beside us.

See for Yourself

Haleakala National Park: *www.nps.gov/hale*

Haleakala, on the island of Maui, is home to more endangered species than any other national park. Among them is Hawaii's state bird, the nene, related to the Canada goose and recognized by its zebra-like stripes. The spiky but fragile silversword plant, with its large purple blooms, grows only on the summit.

That summit can take up to two hours to reach, depending on where you start from, but the drive is well worth it. Stop at the pair of overlooks along the way as well as the Visitor Center (be mindful it may close in mid-afternoon). Bring your own water and snacks, as well as a jacket, because temperatures can dip below freezing at that height. The paths are rocky, so wear sturdy shoes. Go when there's a full moon for a different experience—and bring a flashlight for the path.

You might be curious about an array of buildings you'll see as you climb to the peak. Science City consists of observatories and surveillance systems operated by the United States Air Force and the University of Hawaii, among others.

The park is the world's largest dormant volcano, created not by an eruption but by two valleys merging. It's officially considered active, but hasn't rumbled since 1790. Its ochre and ash-colored crater is three thousand feet deep, seven and a half miles long, and two and a half miles wide—big enough to hold all of Manhattan. You can take a short stroll down into the basin on the Keoneheʻeheʻe (Sliding Sands) Trail. This path traverses the entire crater and connects to the

Halemau'u Trail, which has three cabins and two campgrounds if you want to spend the night. None have electricity or potable water. Reserve spaces for them online. There's also a drive-up campground close to the summit.

If you're looking for a bit of adventure, sign up with one of several nearby bike rental shops for a very early morning drive to the top followed by a thrilling but potentially risky twenty-three mile ride down on two wheels. In your own car, save your brakes and shift into low gear as you descend.

The other side of Haleakala is the lush, green Kipahulu coast. From December to April, seals, dolphins, and humpback whales hang out there. The trip along the infamous Hana Highway can be challenging, and you might consider a bus tour instead of driving yourself. The park has another drive-in campground near the Visitor Center.

As long as you're in the Aloha State, you might as well make the most of it and visit Hawaii Volcanoes National Park on Big Island. The two parks started out as Hawaii National Park in 1916, and were divided into separate units in 1961.

From Fossils to Precious Stones
Petrified Forest National Park

I will give you a new heart and put a new spirit in you; I will remove from you your heart of stone and give you a heart of flesh.

Ezekiel 36:26

Want to see trees that have been transformed into colorful stone? Then plan a visit to Petrified Forest National Park.

Located near the southern edge of the Colorado Plateau in northeastern Arizona, this amazing geographical area has two parts, the forest and the adjacent Painted Desert. The forest used to be a floodplain thick with tall conifers. As volcanic eruptions toppled them, the swollen rivers swept them away. Eventually, layers of silt, mud, and ash buried the trees. Groundwater laden with silica and minerals gradually replaced their wood cells, which slowly crystallized into sparkling quartz. Continental drift caused the land to rise and erosion stripped away the soft sediment layers, revealing the hardened trees.

People became aware of the colorful remains in the mid-1800s, and began to take chunks of the rainbow-hued rocks as souvenirs. President Theodore Roosevelt set aside part of the landscape as the Petrified Forest National Monument in the fall of 1906, and it achieved national park status in 1962. George W. Bush signed legislation in 2004 to more than double its administrative boundary during his presidency.

The above verse from Ezekiel presents a graphic picture of what we might call petrified hearts. Like trees in Petrified Forest, they're not hardened suddenly, but over time, as the sludge, muck, and residue of our inborn mutinous nature build up and entomb our most vital organ.

I'm well acquainted with that unruly disposition and its results. The tug of war between my desires and God's achieves nothing as pretty as the petrified rocks.

Ossified hearts, God warns, are downright ugly, and lead to futility, foolishness, and ultimately destruction. They arouse God's wrath . . . and cause him great grief.

The Petrified Forest illustrates that God can make even fossilized things beautiful. These trees-turned-to-stone look tough, but they are actually brittle and must be handled gently. Our loving Father, who sculpted every bit of creation, understands just how to handle our wayward and so breakable hearts, treating them with loving care. As David says in Psalm 103:14, "He knows how we are formed, he remembers that we are dust." Restoration is his aim; David also acknowledges: "A broken and contrite heart, O God, you will not despise" (Psalm 51:17). He even initiates the process: "I will search for the lost and bring back the strays. I will bind up the injured and strengthen the weak" (Ezekiel 34:16). Taking him up on his offer is as swift and simple as a prayer.

Oh, we'll have to ask again and again for him to crack that hardened shell. Petrified logs are continually heaved up as weather and other forces strip away the dirt. God recognizes our default disposition is toward sin. But his perfect and tender erosion is enough to keep us clean, and form us into what Peter calls living, chosen stones (1 Peter 2:4-5).

One day, all those who call upon the Lord for salvation will receive a "heart transplant." That's when our too-often petrified tickers will be replaced with ones that are permanently unsoiled, soft, and pure. Finally they'll be completely and forever restored by and beating in sync with the Great Physician.

See for Yourself

Petrified Forest National Park: *www.nps.gov/pefo*

Resist the urge to take rock fragments. Instead, purchase legal ones from private land at shops outside the park.

The 93,000-acre park has many places to explore by car or on foot, each one reflecting the climate that shaped it and the people who lived there. Autumn is a good time to visit because of milder temperatures, and October 15 is National Fossil Day!

Many of the trails are short and paved, overlooking the rim of the Painted Desert, lovely Crystal Forest, and ancient pueblo structures. Visitors can see 650 rock carvings, or petroglyphs, on Newspaper Rock from a catwalk equipped with free spotting scopes for a closer view.

The Painted Desert Inn, where legendary "Harvey Girls" once served travelers, doesn't offer meals or accommodations anymore, but is now a museum with the original Hopi Indian murals still intact. What you'll find is an exhibit about the Civilian Conservation Corps, the Depression-era program whose workers constructed many of the building and trails we continue to enjoy in our parks. You'll also learn about Route 66—Petrified Forest is the only park with a swath of the historic roadway running through it.

Up for an epic adventure? Set aside a couple of weeks of vacation in the Four Corners, where Arizona, Colorado, New Mexico, and Nevada meet. Fly into Las Vegas, Albuquerque, or Flagstaff, and travel a huge loop to see not only several Park Service sites, but also many other attractions and incredible scenery in one memorable trip. Highlights in Arizona include Petrified Forest and Grand Canyon National Park, two National Recreation Areas—Lake Mead and Glen Canyon—plus nine National Monuments—Canyon De Chelly, Montezuma Castle, Navajo, Parashant, Pipe Spring, Sunset Crater Volcano, Tuzigoot, Walnut Canyon, and Wupatki. In Colorado, hit Mesa Verde, Black Canyon of the Gunnison, and Great Sand Dunes National Parks, as well as Colorado and Yucca House National Monuments and Curecanti National Recreation Area. The National Monuments of Aztec Ruins, Bandelier, El Malpais, El Morro, Petroglyph, and

Salinas Pueblo Missions are in New Mexico. Utah has Arches, Bryce, Canyonlands, Capitol Reef, and Zion National Parks, and Cedar Breaks, Hovenweep, Natural Bridges, and Rainbow Bridge National Monuments.

And make time to drive through picturesque Monument Valley, on the Arizona/Utah border. The backdrop for many western films, the area is accessible through the Monument Valley Navajo Tribal Park (*www.navajonationparks.org*).

Who's in Charge Here?
American Presidents Sites

The Most High is sovereign over the kingdoms of men and gives them to anyone he wishes.

Daniel 4:17, 25, 32

We greet November with a sigh of relief these days, because it ends the seemingly ceaseless rounds of mudslinging, robocalls, and advertising that accompany every election. The presidential contests held every four years add an extra measure of patience-stretching torment. I've found that one way to catch a break from all the hoopla is to look at campaigns of past presidents.

The National Archives and Records Administration oversees presidential libraries and museums, but the National Park Service has a number of sites devoted to former chief executives. You may be familiar with many, such as the Washington, Jefferson, and Lincoln Memorials in Washington, D.C., but there are others detailing the lives of some of our more obscure leaders—Martin Van Buren, anyone?

You might be reading this after the first Tuesday in November, and already know the outcome of the latest national, state, or local election. Maybe you're pleased that your favorite won, and look forward to better days. Or perhaps you're not so happy because your candidate lost, and you're worried about what this new official is going to do.

In any case, you can be confident of this: they are in office by God's appointment. That message is so important that the book of Daniel declares it three times.

The New Testament continues the theme of God's hand in government and our relationship to it in Titus 3:1, 1 Peter 2:13-17 and, most notably, Romans 13:1-2: "Everyone must submit himself to the governing authorities, for there is no authority except that which God has established. The authorities that exist have been established by God. Consequently, he who rebels against the authority is rebelling against what God has instituted." That God puts rulers—good or bad, pleasing or maddening—in place over us *and* requires us to submit to them can be a challenge.

No, God is not surprised, alarmed, or disappointed in the results of any election. Nothing escapes his purview. He "sits high and looks low," as a pastor friend of mine likes to paraphrase Isaiah 57:15. Scripture assures us he knows exactly what's going on—it's all part of his plan, and his purposes are never thwarted. He has the power to preserve and protect his people and to turn things around for good. We can rest in the fact that God is in charge, despite the circumstances or our feelings.

If you're discouraged about what's going on in Washington, the statehouse, or your own town, fight the urge to disengage. It's our duty and our privilege as earthly—and heavenly—citizens to participate in the government God has set over us. Let's vote, contact our representatives, and make our opinions known. Let's be salt and light, as we bring glory to God by loving our enemies and modeling God's mercy to all. Let's support each other and spread God's message of hope, all while keeping our own conduct above board. Then leave the results to him.

A tall order, to be sure. That's why we first need to talk it all over with the Most High. He's in office for life.

See for Yourself

American Presidents Sites:

www.nps.gov/nr/travel/presidents/list_of_sites.html

Here's where you will find the list of National Park Service locations across the country dedicated to former commanders-in-chief and the places where they spent significant time before, during, or after their terms in office. A sampling:

- Adams National Historical Park in Massachusetts is home to the oldest intact birthplaces of two American presidents, John Adams and his son, John Quincy Adams. (*www.nps.gov/adam*)

- Andrew Johnson had the unfortunate task of following an assassinated predecessor and came close to being impeached, but his story of rising from a poor, nearly illiterate tailor's apprentice is fascinating, as told at the Andrew Johnson National Historic Site in Tennessee. (*www.nps.gov/anjo*)

- The General Grant National Memorial on Manhattan's Upper West Side is where the Civil War commander and eighteenth president is buried, along with his wife. Mosaics depict the battles of Vicksburg and Chattanooga, as well as the surrender at Appomattox. Trophy rooms display Union Army battle flags and mural maps of some of Grant's most important skirmishes. (*www.nps.gov/gegr*)

- Theodore Roosevelt's home on Long Island, New York, at Sagamore Hill National Historic Site, showcases a remarkable collection of objects. They reflect the life of this energetic soldier and politician who became a leader in preserving land for the national parks. (*www.nps.gov/sahi*)

- Our thirty-first president is usually thought of as the hapless one who led us into the Depression. But Iowa's Herbert Hoover National Historic Site details his successful efforts to feed the hungry in Europe after World Wars I and II, a consequence of his strong Quaker faith. (*www.nps.gov/heho*)

- As might be expected of a president who served four terms, Franklin Delano Roosevelt has multiple National Park sites, including one in Canada. His National Memorial is on the Mall in Washington D.C. The Home of Franklin D. Roosevelt National Historic Site is in Hyde Park, New York, two miles away from his wife's place. Val-Kill Cottage at Eleanor Roosevelt National

Historic Site is the only Park site dedicated to a specific First Lady. The Roosevelt Campobello International Park is in New Brunswick, Canada—where he contracted polio, yet spent many happy hours with his family.

FDR Memorial (*www.nps.gov/frde*)
Home of Franklin D. Roosevelt NHS (*www.nps.gov/hofr*)
Eleanor Roosevelt NHS (*www.nps.gov/elro*)
Roosevelt Campobello (*www.nps.gov/roca*)

- Speaking of women in the White House, First Ladies National Historic Site in Canton, Ohio depicts the accomplishments of all the females who held that title. (*www.nps.gov/fila*)

- Dwight Eisenhower deliberately made his home near Gettysburg, Pennsylvania, so visitors can tour the Eisenhower National Historic Site and the Civil War battleground in one trip. (*www.nps.gov/eise*)

- Lyndon B. Johnson National Historical Park in Texas is where this president was born, grew up, planned his political career, and returned to escape the pressures of his various offices. It became his retirement home and burial site as well. (*www.nps.gov/lyjo*)

Sifting Our Hearts
Sites of Remembrance for Veterans Day

I saw heaven standing open and there before me was a white horse, whose rider is called Faithful and True. With justice he judges and makes war...Out of his mouth comes a sharp sword with which to strike down the nations...He treads the winepress of the fury of the wrath of God Almighty. On his robe and on his thigh he has this name written: KING OF KINGS AND LORD OF LORDS.

Revelation 19:11, 15-16

Each November, we pause to honor the men and women who have served our country in the military. The tradition started after World War I, when President Wilson marked the first anniversary of Armistice Day, November 11, the day that hostilities ceased in 1918. Congress made the day a legal United States holiday in 1938, dedicated to those who fought in the "war to end all wars" and to the cause of world peace. The act was amended in 1954 to include service members from all American wars, and replace the word "Armistice" with "Veterans." The Uniform Holiday Bill of 1968, intended to create three-day holiday weekends, moved the event to a Monday, but that created such uproar that President Ford signed legislation to return the observance to its original date. And so it remains.

Since the National Park Service preserves battlefields, military parks, and historic sites related to the many wars our country has fought both within and outside its borders, it offers numerous places to learn more about those episodes in our history. Veterans Day is a perfect time to visit these locations because many hold special events every November 11, and defer entrance fees.

I've been to more Civil War parks than any other war-related ones, probably because there are so many of them (the American Revolution sites run a distant second in number). When I go, I often think of this melancholy tune I learned in elementary school, one popularized during that wrenching struggle:

> *We're tenting tonight on the old campground;*
> *Give us a song to cheer*
> *Our weary hearts, a song of home,*
> *And friends we love so dear.*

> *Many are the hearts that are weary tonight,*
> *Wishing for the war to cease;*
> *Many are the hearts looking for the right*
> *To see the dawn of peace.*

> *Tenting tonight,*
> *Tenting tonight,*
> *Tenting on the old campground.*

> *We've been fighting today on the old campground,*
> *Many are lying near;*
> *Some are dead, some are dying,*
> *Many are in tears.*

> *Dying tonight,*
> *Dying tonight,*
> *Dying on the old campground.*

Most songs from that era are tinged with sadness, as might be expected, with the notable exception of the rousing "When Johnny Comes Marching Home Again." Perhaps the most memorable and recognizable piece of music to come out of the time is "The Battle Hymn of the Republic":

Mine eyes have seen the glory of the coming of the Lord,
He is trampling out the vintage where the grapes of wrath are stored;
He hath loosed the fateful lightning of His terrible swift sword,
His truth is marching on.

I have seen Him in the watchfires of a hundred circling camps,
They have builded Him an altar in the evening dews and damps;
I can read His righteous sentence by the dim and flaring lamps,
His day is marching on.

He has sounded forth the trumpet that shall never call retreat,
He is sifting out the hearts of men before His judgment seat;
O be swift, my soul, to answer Him, be jubilant, my feet!
Our God is marching on.

In the beauty of the lilies Christ was born across the sea,
With a glory in His being that transfigures you and me;
As He died to make men holy let us live to make men free!
While God is marching on.

Glory! Glory! Hallelujah!
Glory! Glory! Hallelujah!
Glory! Glory! Hallelujah!
His truth is marching on!

Revelation 19 inspired Julia Ward Howe to pen these lyrics, with the melody borrowed from "John Brown's Body." That refrain, about the pre-Civil War abolitionist, was set to a tune from the nineteenth-century American Christian camp meeting movement. The song links the end-times judgment and Jesus's final war with Satan with the Civil War.

These days, in a less Bible-literate culture, "The Battle Hymn of the Republic" is seen mainly as a patriotic song, one that is sometimes frowned upon because of its war-like imagery. The Christian reference and meaning has been lost in the shuffle.

Make no mistake: just as there was a four-year long war that threatened to forever tear apart the Union, in the future there will be the biggest battle ever seen—the ultimate clash between good and evil, between those who have believed and received Jesus as their Savior, and those who have actively rejected or indifferently ignored him.

Matthew 25 and Revelation 20 elaborate on this "sifting out" of hearts. Like being a Confederate at the end of the Civil War, there is no happy ending for those found on the losing side of this last, epic fight. "If anyone's name was not found written in the book of life, he was thrown into the lake of fire" (Revelation 20:15).

God's final verdict will be sharp, fierce, and decisive, but also just and true, because he is the ultimate Judge over all. He has patiently invited us to seek and find him, giving us plenty of warning of what is to come.

Celebrating those who served to unite our nation and secure our freedom is a good thing to do. My prayer is that you'll also make sure your eternal future is secure as well, paid for by Jesus's death and resurrection. That's a freedom far beyond what any war could ever accomplish.

See for Yourself

Sites of Remembrance for Veterans Day:
www.nps.gov/findapark/military-remember.htm

As the Park Service notes, "What better way to honor those who served their country than to visit a national park that preserves the places where they fought?"

This web page links to memorials, parks, and battlefields across the nation where history was made in not only the Revolutionary War, Civil War, and World War II, but also in lesser-known but still significant conflicts like the French & Indian War, the War of 1812, the Mexican-American War, and the American Indian Wars.

Short but Sweet
Gettysburg National Military Park

When I came to you, I did not come with eloquence or superior wisdom as I proclaimed to you the testimony about God. For I resolved to know nothing while I was with you except Jesus Christ and him crucified...My message and my preaching were not with wise and persuasive words, but with a demonstration of the Spirit's power, so that your faith might not rest on men's wisdom, but on God's power.

1 Corinthians 2:1-2, 4-5

The three-day encounter between Union and Confederate forces at Gettysburg occurred in early July, but November 19 is another notable date at the site because it marks one of history's most memorable speeches.

Following that momentous battle of 1863, a temporary cemetery was set up on a town hillside to bury many of the dead, until prominent citizens became concerned about the poor condition of the graves. Eventually Gettysburg lawyer David Wills was appointed to coordinate the establishment of a soldiers' cemetery; removal of the Union dead began that fall. The Confederate remains were moved to the South, with most interred in Richmond, Virginia.

First there had to be a dedication of the new burial site. Wills invited President Abraham Lincoln to provide concluding remarks following the main address by well-known orator Edward Everett. This wasn't a slight to the president, as Everett was renowned for his public speaking. And he had other impressive credentials: he was an ordained minister who received his education at Harvard, and later taught at and was president of that institution. He served in both chambers of Congress, as well as serving as a governor of Massachusetts and an envoy to Great Britain. He was Secretary of State under Millard Fillmore, and ran as an unsuccessful vice presidential candidate in 1860.

Everett's speech to the approximately fifteen thousand who attended the ceremony lasted two hours, not an unusual length according to the style of the time. President Lincoln also was known for long speeches, but on that day, he spoke briefly:

> Four score and seven years ago our fathers brought forth on this continent, a new nation, conceived in liberty, and dedicated to the proposition that all men are created equal. Now, we are engaged in a great civil war, testing whether that nation, or any nation so conceived and so dedicated, can long endure. We are met on a great battlefield of that war. We have come to dedicate a portion of that field, as a final resting-place for those who here gave their lives that that nation might live. It is altogether fitting and proper that we should do this. But, in a larger sense, we can not dedicate— we can not consecrate—we can not hallow this ground. The brave men, living and dead, who struggled here have consecrated it, far above our poor power to add or detract. The world will little note, nor long remember what we say here, but it can never forget what they did here. It is for us the living, rather, to be dedicated here to the unfinished work which they who fought here have thus far so

nobly advanced. It is rather for us to be here dedicated to the great task remaining before us—that from these honored dead we take increased devotion to that cause for which they gave the last full measure of devotion—that we here highly resolve that these dead shall not have died in vain—that this nation, under God, shall have a new birth of freedom—and that government of the people, by the people, and for the people shall not perish from the earth.

Note: Contrary to popular lore, Lincoln didn't whip up his remarks on the back of an envelope. He wrote at least half on White House stationery before his trip to Pennsylvania, and apparently finished it at the Wills house, where he and Everett both stayed the night of November 18. The Library of Congress notes there are five known manuscripts of what's come to be known as the Gettysburg Address—it has two, one from each of Lincoln's private secretaries.

Everett sent Lincoln a short note the following day, asking for a copy of the speech. He wrote: "Permit me also to express my great admiration of the thoughts expressed by you, with such eloquent simplicity & appropriateness at the consecration of the Cemetery. I should be glad, if I could flatter myself that I came as near to the central idea of the occasion, in two hours, as you did in two minutes." (Library of Congress, 1995). Lincoln obliged, and Everett's copy resides at the Illinois State Historical Library; the final two copies are at Cornell University and in the Lincoln Room at the White House.

Lincoln didn't require many words to capture the feelings of a torn country that fall day. Nor do we need many words to communicate the Bible's central message, as the apostle Paul reiterated in his letter to the Corinthian church. It is, he said, actually a very simple one, perhaps best expressed in one of the most beloved and well-known passages of Scripture: "For God so loved the world that he gave his one and only Son, that whoever believes in him shall not perish but have eternal life."

Sure, God could have provided us with much more information, but he chose not to. As the apostle John concluded in his gospel, "Jesus did many other things as well. If every one of them were written down, I suppose that even the whole world would not have room for the books that would be written."

What we do have is the assurance that we have everything we need to live a life pleasing to God. We don't know it all, but we know the powerful God who does.

It's a short, sweet message the world is dying to hear.

See for Yourself

Gettysburg National Military Park: *www.nps.gov/gett*

Dedication Day ceremonies are held annually each November 19, and include a wreath laying ceremony at the Soldiers' National Cemetery.

For any visit, stop first at the Museum and Visitor Center. There's an admission fee to the Gettysburg Museum Experience at the center. Ranger-led programs to the battlefield and the cemetery are free and conducted mid-June through mid-August. The walks range from twenty minutes to two hours in length. Or pick up a no-cost self-guided auto tour to explore at your own pace.

Other audio tours are available for purchase at the park bookstore, and bus excursions with licensed battlefield guides can be booked for a fee. Winter brings a lecture series on topics related to the Civil War.

In the town of Gettysburg itself, consider visiting the David Wills House, which charges admission.

Winter

Redeeming the Season
Wolf Trap National Park for the Performing Arts

> *See to it that no one takes you captive through hollow and deceptive philosophy, which depends on human tradition and the basic principles of this world rather than on Christ.*

1 Corinthians 2:1-2, 4-5

If you're reading this during December, chances are your mind is already working overtime thinking about end-of-the-year activities, meals, travel plans, and above all, what to buy for everyone on your list. Maybe the vague apprehension hit way back in August, when Christmas items began crowding out the Halloween decorations, and has been slowly building ever since.

Yeah, I feel it, too.

The problem, of course, is that there are so many things to do during the season that only happen once a year, and we drive ourselves nuts trying to fit them all in. So…let me tell you about one more!

Wolf Trap National Park for the Performing Arts, about twenty miles west of Washington, D.C., has the distinction of being the only unit of the National Park Service solely dedicated to presenting the performing arts. Over one hundred dance, theatre, and music productions are put on May through September in its outdoor amphitheaters.

The first Saturday in December brings the annual Wolf Trap Holiday Sing-a-Long. This celebration includes a concert by the United States Marine Band as well as group singing of Christmas carols, Hanukkah tunes, and other seasonal melodies accompanied by local choir and vocal groups. A traditional candle lighting ceremony and singing of "Silent Night" top off the evening.

Whenever I hear the word *tradition*, I think of the musical *Fiddler on the Roof* and its opening number, probably because I sang it what seems like a million times during my days in summer stock theatre. The show opens with a few notes of a haunting melody from a man sitting on a rooftop playing a violin. Over the music, the main character, Tevye, addresses the audience, declaring that he and his fellow townspeople are like that fiddler, each "trying to scratch out a pleasant, simple tune without breaking his neck." The way they keep their balance, he says, is by tradition. The chorus of townspeople emphatically agrees by belting out, "Tradition!" several times.

Tevye mentions that many of their customs reflect their devotion to God, especially the wearing of a head covering and prayer shawl. He doesn't know how these practices started, but "it's a tradition!"

The village fathers, mothers, sons, and daughters go on to sing of their established roles. Yes, tradition is the glue that holds them together and helps them get along, Tevye says, just before an argument breaks out. The song ends with Tevye concluding that without traditions, their lives would be as precarious as…a fiddler on the roof. The story then unfolds to break every tradition the song mentions.

Tradition is a loaded term around holidays, especially religious ones. "But we've always done it this way!" and "It's just not Christmas if we don't (fill in the blank)" become the watchwords. They can make what should be an enjoyable, uncomplicated observance of Jesus's birth into a wobbly balancing act that often leaves us as stressed and shaky as…a fiddler on the roof.

How did we wind up snared in rituals that seemed like good ideas in the past, but now just amp up the pressure? More importantly, why do we do this to ourselves? The must-do list gets longer and longer, time flies, the credit card receipts pile up, and suddenly…oh by the way, happy birthday, Jesus.

Can we put a stop to this madness and take back the essence of Christmas? Absolutely. Not only should we for the sake of our own sanity, but for the sake of the gospel as well.

Jesus's stinging rebuke of the Pharisees and teachers of the law in Mark 7:6-8 is as relevant today as it was then. He said, "Isaiah was right when he prophesied about you hypocrites; as it is written: 'These people honor me with their lips, but their hearts are far from me. They worship me in vain; their teachings are but rules taught by men.'" He ends with this pointed zinger: "You have let go of the commands of God and are holding on to the traditions of men."

Does this mean we should give up gift giving, parties, and sing-a-longs? Not necessarily. But the question we need to ask is, "Are my traditions pointing me, my family, and/or others to Jesus?" If the answer is no, then it's time to seriously consider why we're doing them.

Tradition! Are you serving it, or is it serving Christ? This December, join me in reexamining every "must do," letting go of the ones that are deceptively hollow, and embracing those that draw us closer to the baby in the manger.

See for Yourself

Wolf Trap National Park for the Performing Arts:
www.nps.gov/wotr

The free Sing-a-Long is very popular, so if you decide to attend, plan to arrive well before the 4:00 p.m. start time to take advantage of the complimentary but limited parking. Bring your own candle for lighting and, if you'd like, a bell to play for the "Jing-a-Long" during the singing of "Jingle Bells." New, unwrapped toys are collected at the entrance for the Toys for Tots program.

During the warmer months, the two venues in the park, the Filene Center and Theatre-in-the Woods, stay busy with a wide range of performances in a variety of genres. Pack a picnic, then wander in the woods along either of the park's two trails before or after a show.

Come to the Banquet
Yosemite National Park

He has taken me to the banquet hall, and his banner over me is love.

Song of Songs 2:4

Wildlife, great scenery, trails...those are the things most of us imagine when we think of the national parks. Yosemite, of course, has all that. What it also has is an annual Christmas pageant.

For close to a century, Yosemite's Ahwahnee Hotel, a National Historic Landmark, has hosted the Bracebridge Dinner. The hotel's log-beamed dining room—with massive stone hearths, Native American artwork, and gorgeous stained glass—is transformed into an eighteenth-century English manor hall for a festival of food, song, and ceremony.

The hours-long affair, held several times during December, incorporates Renaissance rituals, caroling, and a sumptuous meal. More than a hundred people participate in the show, based on

Washington Irving's novel *Bracebridge Hall*, portraying the Squire of the castle and his family, their servants, minstrels, and other performers. This yearly holiday tradition has continued since 1927, interrupted only by floods and war, and evidently is very popular, despite its hefty cost. Dinner-only tickets are around $400 per person.

The Bracebridge dinner reminds me of the parable of the wedding banquet, found in Matthew 22:1-14 and Luke 14:16-24, one of several parables in which Jesus talks about the kingdom of heaven. Only in the book of Matthew is the phrase, "kingdom of heaven" used (and it's mentioned thirty-two times), and refers to the spiritual rule of God in the hearts of those who put their trust in Jesus.

In this parable, a king planned a feast in honor of his son's wedding. As was the custom in Bible times, he not only sent out advance invitations, but on the day of the dinner also directed messengers to escort the guests in. Everything was ready—but the invitees wouldn't come. They gave excuses like, "I have just bought a field, and I must go and see it," and "I have just bought five yoke of oxen, and I'm on my way to try them out," and "I just got married, so I can't come" (Luke 14:18-20). Matthew even says that some of the invited guests went so far as to kill the messengers.

The king was furious. To refuse an invitation at the last minute was just not done in that culture. To kill an innocent person for no reason at all was inexcusable. In response, the king sent out his army to destroy the murderers and their city.

But there was still the matter of the wedding celebration. "Then [the king] said to his servants, 'The wedding banquet is ready, but those I invited did not deserve to come. Go to the street corners and invite to the banquet anyone you find.' So the servants went out into the streets and gathered all the people they could find, both good and bad" (Matthew 22:8-10). When the hall had room for still more, the king sent them out again to scour all the main roads and even the country lanes and make people come in.

That's kind of like walking along in London in your everyday clothes and suddenly a palace attendant asks you to join the Queen and her family at a party!

Do you know what my concern would be? That I wasn't prepared. That I didn't have a nice dress on, and certainly didn't have a present on hand that was worthy of royalty.

The king in this parable thought of that, too. He didn't supply a present, but he distributed appropriate attire, because he knew the average person wouldn't have a suitable outfit.

Curiously, one guest didn't avail himself of the new clothes. He had been invited and provided for, and wanted to be part of the fun, the excitement, and the honor, but he wanted to do so on his own terms. When pressed by the king as to why he hadn't put on the offered wedding clothes, the man had no explanation. As a result, Matthew relates that the king's attendants tossed the stubborn invitee out into the darkness, where he had plenty of time to rue his decision. Jesus ends the parable with this admonition: "For many are invited, but few are chosen" (Matthew 22:14).

Yosemite's Bracebridge dinner doesn't send out invitations. Anybody can attend—as long as he or she can afford it, and the reservations aren't all taken. The ever-gracious God summons the entire world to enjoy his presence, all at no cost—his Son has already paid the entrance fee. Yet he knows some will be indifferent to the call, or make excuses, or even be downright hostile.

God never gives up inviting. As the king appealed to both the good and the bad, God doesn't care what you've done, where you've been, or what you do or don't have. He's not asking you to spruce yourself up before joining him, and he's not looking for you to give him anything except yourself. He just wants you to *come*! *He'll* clean you up, with his "garments of salvation [and] robe of righteousness" (Isaiah 61:10).

The question is—have you answered the compelling invitation of a gracious King?

I hope to see you at the table. I'll save you a seat.

See for Yourself

Yosemite National Park: *www.nps.gov/yose*

The winter season is Yosemite's best-kept secret—less people, accessible roads, and many open trails. Snow sports abound. Take the bus from nearby Merced, and you won't even have to worry about driving.

If Horsetail Fall is flowing in mid- to late February, you're in for a treat. As the sun goes down, the waterfall blazes with reds and oranges, making the water look like fire falling from El Capitan.

The summer months are very busy, and you have to book at least several months ahead for any of the park's accommodations. Leave your car in the lot and take the park shuttle to get where you want to go, or rent bikes.

The 2.4-mile round trip hike to Vernal Fall is strenuous, with over six hundred granite stairs at the end, but the lovely waterfall and Emerald Pool make it worthwhile. Bridalveil and Lower Yosemite Falls have easier trails, as does Mirror Lake, which is a great place to spot wildlife. The Cook's Meadow Loop has a classic view of Half Dome and many other formations.

For a different perspective on the park's famous landmarks, consider a nighttime tour during evenings when the moon is full.

Due to pending trademark litigation at the time of this writing, the Ahwahnee Hotel might be rechristened the Majestic Yosemite Hotel. The name may change, but the facility will remain its luxurious self.

No Condemnation
World War II Valor in the Pacific
National Monument

There is therefore now no condemnation for those who are in Christ Jesus.

Romans 8:1

My husband always scans the obituaries. Since both his parents served in the armed forces during World War II, he pays special attention to the deaths of this war's veterans as their numbers rapidly dwindle. A few years ago, he pointed out a notice he thought would interest me.

"'Don't worry about it,'" began the obit. "Those words, which he uttered on a peaceful Sunday morning in 1941 on the Hawaiian island of Oahu, would haunt Kermit A. Tyler for the rest of his life."

On December 7 of that year, Mr. Tyler was a first lieutenant for the Army Air Force on temporary duty in Honolulu, at Fort Shafter's radar information center. He received a report from a radar operator further north of a large "blip" on the screen, which seemed to indicate numerous aircraft approaching rapidly.

"Don't worry about it," Tyler told the radar operator. He thought it was probably an expected flight of United States B-17 bombers coming in.

As you might have guessed, that "blip" wasn't from American aircraft—it was the first wave of Japanese planes sent to attack Pearl Harbor, sparking our country's entry into the Second World War.

The newspaper piece noted that Mr. Tyler's four-word sentence lived on in history books, articles, and even the 1970 movie about the surprise assault, *Tora! Tora! Tora!* "Audiences watching the Pearl Harbor documentary at the Pearl Harbor Visitor Center still groan when they hear Tyler's response," the article relates and mentions that Tyler was often ridiculed and second-guessed over the years. He even received letters reviling him for not taking action that infamous day.

But Daniel Martinez, chief historian for the National Park Service's World War II Valor in the Pacific National Monument, of which Pearl Harbor is a part, defended the young officer. "He was never trained for that job," he's quoted as saying. "He had a walk-through the previous Wednesday, but had never spent a full day there." Even Congressional and military inquiries didn't find him at fault.

What about Mr. Tyler himself? Did he live in misery over the last sixty-eight years of his life, adversely affected by his actions and words? Apparently not. He flew combat missions during the war, retired from the Air Force as a lieutenant colonel, earned a business degree, and worked in real estate. He married and had children, grandchildren, and even a great-grandchild.

Did his past really haunt him, as the article claims? Not according to an interview he gave to New Jersey's *Star Ledger* in 2007. "I wake up at nights sometimes and think about it," he said. "But I don't feel guilty. I did all I could that morning."

I admire a man involved in such a momentous historic event, who was still able to have the proper perspective of his role in it, even when others maligned him. When I think of how I berate myself for my mistakes, omissions, and instances where, like Mr. Tyler's, I did all I could yet the outcome wasn't good…well, they just can't begin to equal what he went through.

And they pale in comparison to what Jesus did for not only me, but also for Mr. Tyler and the rest. By dying on the cross, he paid the price for all the blame I rightly—and wrongly—put on myself:

"You have put all my sins behind your back." (Isaiah 38:17)

"'I, even I, am he who blots out your transgressions, for my own sake, and remembers your sins no more.'" (Isaiah 43:25)

"'I have swept away your offenses like a cloud, your sins like the morning mist.'" (Isaiah 44:22)

"Who is a God like you, who pardons sin and forgives the transgression of the remnant of his inheritance? You do not stay angry forever but delight to show mercy. You will again have compassion on us; you will tread our sins underfoot and hurl all our iniquities into the depths of the sea." (Micah 7:18-19)

"Repent, then, and turn to God, so that your sins may be wiped out, that times of refreshing may come from the Lord." (Acts 3:19)

"God forgave us all our sins, having canceled the written code, with its regulations, that was against us and that stood opposed to us; he took it away, nailing it to the cross." (Colossians 2:13-14)

What a wonderful word picture these verses paint! The Lord has taken all the offenses we've ever done or will do, and infinitely separated them from us. He stamped "Paid In Full" on that sin debt by putting it on Jesus, who took the punishment we justifiably deserved.

Then he forgets there even was any wrongdoing to begin with!

How he does that, I don't know. I can't begin to wrap my mind around the notion. But I figure that if he's great enough to create the world, then he's great enough to disremember. Still, unlike Mr. Tyler, I regularly beat myself up about my mistakes and failures, whether they were my fault or not, and too often I suppose that's what God must do too. Yet when he casts our sins into the ocean, he declares it off-limits to fishing. Because as far as he's concerned, and as incredible as it seems, there's nothing there.

Now that *is* something to remember.

See for Yourself

World War II Valor in the Pacific National Monument:
www.nps.gov/valr

This park, signed into existence by President George W. Bush in 2008, includes nine locations in Hawaii, Alaska, and California. All cover different aspect of the war, but the most popular and well-known site is Pearl Harbor in Hawaii.

Here visitors can take in the USS *Arizona* Memorial and USS *Bowfin* Submarine Museum & Park, as well as the Battlefield *Missouri*

Memorial and Pacific Aviation Museum on Ford Island, accessible via shuttle. You can reserve free tickets for the *Arizona* up to two months in advance, and an audio tour of the entire site is available for a fee. Security is tight.

Light and Life
Antietam National Battlefield

In Jesus was life, and the life was the light of men.

John 1:4

If you see a large glow in the sky over Sharpsburg, Maryland on the first Sunday in December, don't be alarmed. It's just the luminarias.

Every year on that day, Antietam National Battlefield sets out sand-and-candle-filled bags to honor the casualties of the bloodiest one-day battle in American military history.

Care to guess how many?

Over twenty-three thousand. All set out for the estimated number of Union and Confederate soldiers killed, maimed, or missing on September 17, 1862.

A staggering number, isn't it?

The twelve-hour savage combat engaged nearly one hundred thousand men and concluded with Confederate General Robert E. Lee withdrawing back across the Potomac River to Virginia, ending his first invasion of the North.

I imagine the Union Army must have seen the battle as a good news/bad news sort of triumph. So horrible a fight, so many lost. If they'd known the war was going to continue for another two-and-a-half years, they might have been further disheartened. Yet a major victory had been won.

That wasn't all. Lee's retreat gave President Lincoln the opening he'd been waiting for to issue the preliminary Emancipation Proclamation ending slavery.

Why use luminarias to honor the victims of Antietam every December? Perhaps because light has always been associated with Christmas.

According to FLIC Luminaries' history page, convention holds that these illuminations lit the way for Mary and Joseph as they searched for a place to stay before Jesus's birth. Some believe it goes back even further, to the Jewish holiday of Hanukkah, also known as the Festival of Lights.

Spanish settlers introduced *farolitos*, or little lanterns, in the 1500s, lighting small bonfires along roads and in churchyards to commemorate Jesus's birth. The Native American Pueblos set fires to show the way to church on Christmas Eve, a custom still carried out today in Cajun culture. German and French immigrants in Louisiana positioned huge blazes along the Mississippi River in the nineteenth century to "guide" Papa Noel, the Acadian version of Santa, to their houses. In Europe, many people put out luminarias around January 6, the Festival of the Three Kings, signifying the star that led the wise men to Jesus.

Gradually, in this country, people began hanging Chinese lanterns in their doorways instead of building bonfires. Then they started using paper bags as a less expensive alternative.

Light is a central theme in Advent, the four Sundays before Christmas. An Advent wreath holds four candles in its circle—the Prophecy Candle (purple), the Bethlehem Candle (purple), the Shepherd Candle (pink), and the Angel Candle (purple)—each signifying a part of the Christmas story. A white taper in the middle represents Jesus, whom the apostle John, in the first chapter of his gospel, describes as "the true light." Jesus called himself "the light of the world" who provides "the light of life" to all who follow him, so they wouldn't remain in darkness (John 8:12, 12:46).

Perhaps the reason light is such an integral part of Christmas is that the Savior came at a bleak time for the nation of Israel. Four hundred years passed between the events of the Old and New Testaments. I'm sure God's people wondered when the Messianic prophesies were going to be fulfilled. Many passed on, disappointed never to see that day.

Yet God was still at work during those so-called "silent years." The Septuagint, the Greek translation of the Old Testament, was completed then. Antiochus Epiphanes defiled the Temple in Jerusalem by sacrificing swine on the altar; two years later, Judas Maccabeus cleansed it, concluding with the miracle of the oil, now marked by the celebration of Hanukkah. Herod the Great began rebuilding the Temple.

What the Israelites undoubtedly craved during those years was some word, some revelation from God. And when that light came, that "good news of great joy," it was in the most incredible way: God himself in human form, an astounding occurrence after so many years of darkness.

The soldiers who died at Antietam never knew how much good their sacrifice accomplished, just as generations of Israelites never lived to see the Messiah Jesus.

We today have the extraordinary blessing of seeing him—he comes alive to us in the Scriptures, "the word of the prophets made more certain" (2 Peter 1:19), through the intercession he continually makes for us, and through the Holy Spirit he left us.

When we light candles and luminarias in this oftentimes-gloomy world, we memorialize the good news amid the bad, that Jesus was born, lived, and died for us. He emancipated us from our bondage to sin, that we might receive our full rights as his children, no longer slaves, but rightful heirs.

Enjoy the luminarias wherever you find them this December. Like the fires and lanterns of days long ago, let their warm glow lead you again to the Savior whose light pierces even the darkest of days.

Hail the heaven-born Prince of Peace! Hail the Sun of Righteousness!
Light and Life to all He brings, Risen with healing in His wings.
Mild He lays His glory by, Born that man no more may die;
Born to raise the sons of earth, Born to give them second birth.
Hark, the herald angels sing, "Glory to the newborn King."

Charles Wesley

See for Yourself

Antietam National Battlefield: *www.nps.gov/anti*

Volunteers place the luminarias along a five-mile route through the park, and cars may enter beginning at 6:00 p.m. There's no charge. It's a popular area event, and the wait time can be up to two hours. If you can't get there, the website posts a video explaining how it's done, with panoramic shots of what the illumination looks like.

Don't neglect visiting during the day, though. View the introductory film narrated by James Earl Jones at the Visitor Center, then step outside to experience the battlefields and their memorials for yourself. A self-guided auto tour has eleven stops, and several trails of varying lengths allow you to follow in the footsteps of Civil War soldiers.

In the Bleak Midwinter
Morristown National Historical Park

Endure hardship like a good soldier of Christ Jesus.
2 Timothy 2:3

Weather historians agree the winter of 1779-80 was the worst winter of the eighteenth century in New Jersey. And that was very unfortunate for the Continental Army camped around Morristown.

About the best that could be said of the circumstances was that the location was good. It was ideally situated a two days' march from the British base in New York City, and the nearby Watchung Mountains and Great Swamp provided natural defenses. Roads connecting New England and the revolutionary capital at Philadelphia were easily guarded. The water supply was ample, and trees for fuel and construction abundant. Local homes could be used as quarters for generals and staff officers.

Anticipating a long stay in the area, General Washington ordered log huts built to house the enlisted men. Eleven infantry brigades—over ten thousand soldiers—felled more than six hundred acres of oak, walnut, and chestnut to build over a thousand crude shelters.

At least twenty snowstorms impeded the work. For almost all of December, the army slept under tents or with no covering at all. Many were not under roofs until February.

In addition to not having proper shelter, everyone—there were many wives and children accompanying their husbands and fathers—suffered from a lack of food and clothing because snow cut off supply lines. Not that the Continental Congress was doing such a great job of funding the army anyway. "[T]he monster hunger still attended us," one private bitterly noted. "Here was the army starved and naked, and there their country sitting still and expecting the army to do notable things."

Morristown National Historical Park in New Jersey shares the story of those long-ago soldiers and their extraordinary fortitude. Perhaps it's fitting that this place became our country's first park given that designation because, as its official handbook notes:

> The encampments of the Continental Army at Morristown, New Jersey, sum up much of the Revolutionary War. [It] was a war more of waiting than of battles and fighting. For the patriots, perhaps this was just as well, because they tended to lose the battles. But waiting imposed its own trials on patience and the ability of the infant United States and its weak economy to sustain an army in the field. In a contest of patience and endurance, Great Britain might have retained her American empire simply by persisting longer in the struggle than the often impatient patriots. Morristown tested the emotional and physical resources on which depended the Continental Army and ultimately the American cause.

Relief finally came in May of 1780, not only with better weather, but also in the person of the Marquis de Lafayette, who bore the good news that France would be providing military aid. The camp dispersed in June, and the struggle for independence continued.

Scripture often uses the analogy of soldiering and fighting to describe the Christian life. Second Timothy calls us to bear up under adversity, and to be a single-minded and disciplined combatant as we serve our Commanding Officer.

Where would we as a nation be if those brave Continental Army soldiers—who did indeed go on to do "notable things"—had not remained loyal to the cause? In the midst of terrible conditions, they waited out the greatest nation in the world. They kept on going despite great privation, even though they must have wondered at times if the effort was worth it. Now, of course, we know that it was.

Soldiers never know what will happen when they go to war—injury, death, and defeat dog their every step. Very few escape unscathed. Really, the same is true of civilian life.

Perhaps in this season of life, nearly 240 years after those stalwart individuals froze in Morristown, you find yourself in the midst of your own icy spiritual, physical, or emotional chill of suffering and want, not at all certain how it's going to turn out. Take a lesson from these courageous fighters, certainly—but more importantly, look further back in history to Jesus. He did what George Washington could never do: he offered himself as the sacrifice for the sin, sorrow, and sickness of the entire world.

Our Commander doesn't leave us to face our battles alone. He gave us his Holy Spirit to empower us for the fight, and he battles alongside us.

Victory? Guaranteed. "Here is a trustworthy saying: If we died with him, we also live with him; if we endure, we will also reign with him. If we disown him, he will also disown us; if we are faithless, he will remain faithful, for he cannot disown himself" (2 Timothy 2:11-13).

Soldier on.

See for Yourself

Morristown National Historical Park: *www.nps.gov/morr*

Trails and a drivable loop road wind through this site in northern New Jersey, allowing you to enjoy natural beauty while reacquainting yourself with Revolutionary War history at encampment sites, Washington's headquarters, and other historic buildings. At the museum, which charges a fee, you'll find displays on eighteenth century domestic life as well as military and camp life artifacts. The thirty-minute documentary, *Morristown: Where America Survived*, shows there and at the Jockey Hollow Visitor Center.

Because the Garden State figured so prominently in our War of Independence, the Park Service partners with state and local government and organizations to promote the Crossroads of the American Revolution National Heritage Area, an area spread about 2,155 square miles in fourteen counties. For more information, go to *www.revolutionarynj.org*.

What's in a Name?
Death Valley National Park

O Lord, our Lord, how majestic is your name in all the earth!
Psalm 8:1

There are many adjectives used to describe Death Valley—largest (of the national parks in the continental United States), hottest (temps regularly run above 120 degrees in the summer), driest (with an average rainfall of less than two inches annually), and lowest (Badwater Basin, at 282 feet below sea level, is the lowest elevation in North America). But don't assume the park is all desert and nothing else. You'll also find bighorn sheep, cottonwood groves, canyons, wild horses, and a spring-fed waterfall among the four mountain ranges that ring the valley.

Perhaps the question most people ask about Death Valley is how did it get its name? As the story goes, a group of pioneers on their way to California for the Gold Rush got lost there during the winter of 1849-50. Although only one among them perished, the others were afraid they would die there as well. After they finally climbed over the Panamint Mountains to safety, one of the men looked back and said, "Goodbye, Death Valley," and the moniker stuck.

The jewel of this park, according to its website, is the lovely—and pricey—Furnace Creek Inn. The Spanish-style hacienda is nestled against the Funeral (!) Mountains, offering a swimming pool, tennis courts, and a spa. There are televisions with cable in every room, a rarity among national park lodgings. I'd say the amenities are more than enough to take your mind off the extreme conditions.

When I read about the inn, I thought about how its name contrasts with its luxurious description. In every society, names are significant. Consider the importance we attach to them. We agonize over the right one for our children, something unique and meaningful yet not so crazy that they'll be made fun of. Our surnames usually come from ancestors who were tagged according to their habits, characteristics, or jobs.

What about these phrases? A "name brand" is special. When someone "makes a name" for him- or herself, it means they're well known. Both products and people then have to "live up" to their name.

Names carry a lot of weight. They stand for something—an identity, a reputation—and as such are not to be taken lightly.

Scripture likewise attaches meaning to names, often given to reflect a person's character or circumstances of birth, good or bad, such as with Jacob's sons in Genesis chapters 29 and 30.

Names also mark events: think Galeed, which means "heap of witness," and Mizpah, or "watchtower," where Laban and Jacob piled stones as a witness to their wary nonaggression pact, as noted in Genesis 31:44-55.

Of course, God and his Son, Jesus, have many names, or designations, which are easy to look up in a reference Bible or online search. All reflect their distinctive qualities and attributes.

I saw a church sign that read, "Making Jesus Famous." It gave me a chuckle, because "famous" seems an odd word to use. To me, it sounds like the church thinks Jesus needs a public relations boost.

My guess is the sign is referencing John 12:32, where Jesus says that through his death and resurrection—his being "lifted up" on the cross and from the grave—he will draw people to himself. What the church undoubtedly is trying to communicate is that because so many have disregarded Jesus, it's dedicated itself to the task of continually proclaiming his name. No argument from me there! Making him "famous" is just the...*unique* way that church conveys the message, I suppose.

Scripture says that one day his name will be unforgettable. Philippians 2:9-11 tells us that Jesus's name will soar above all others, and at the mere sound of it, every single person will fall down in awe and worship to declare his truth.

Then the God who calls us each by name will exchange it for another, as we transform from sinful to holy, "into his likeness with every increasing glory" (2 Corinthians 3:18). Our new name will have indescribable depth and meaning, perfectly reflecting who we are in him, and "known only to him who receives it" (Revelation 2:17).

Can't wait to hear mine!

See for Yourself

Death Valley National Park: *www.nps.gov/deva*

While the park is open all year, winter brings cooler temperatures—the nights can be downright chilly—which makes hiking much safer and bearable. The week between Christmas and New Year's, Martin Luther King Day weekend in January, and Presidents' Day weekend in February are peak visiting periods. Accommodation reservations are suggested for those times.

Most Death Valley trails are unconstructed, meaning footing can be rough and rocky. But don't let that stop you from taking on the short hikes to salt flats and colorful canyons. If in doubt, check with a ranger. Even better, attend a scheduled program first to get acclimated. Jeep excursions offer a way to see the backcountry without damaging your own car. Don't skip the tour of Scotty's Castle and its underground tunnels.

Whatever you do, bring—and drink—at least two liters of water in the winter and one gallon in the warmer seasons, because of the dry climate.

The Furnace Creek Inn isn't the only lodging available. There are several much less expensive alternatives for sleeping and eating both within and outside the park, along with several campgrounds.

Have Fun but Don't Die
Everglades National Park

> *You have made known to me the path of life; you fill me with joy in*
> *your presence, with eternal pleasures at your right hand.*
>
> Psalm 16:11

Many people believe Everglades National Park is a swamp, but it's not. Swamps are stagnant, and the water in this national park moves steadily out to Florida Bay. Marjory Stoneman Douglas, a journalist who fought hard to protect the over 1.5 million-acre park, the largest subtropical wilderness in the United States, called it a "River of Grass," a fitting description of the aquatic plants undulating in the slow-moving water.

Within this World Heritage Site are about twenty endangered species, including the elusive Florida panther, as well as a multitude of other living things—some that belong, and others that don't. Among the latter is the Burmese python. Thousands have invaded the Everglades, likely the offspring of cast-off pets, and they're threatening the environment by eating the indigenous wildlife, including alligators (think what *that* must look like!). The public has become so fascinated with the snakes that they're becoming a tourist attraction. Gators, birds, and other animals that used to be the star attractions at the park are now ceding the spotlight to creatures that aren't even supposed to be there.

On the other hand are the park's native elements, some of which also pose dangers. A few winters ago, my husband and I were part of a group on a leisurely bicycle ride along the Long Pine Key Trail. Everglades is a place where going off-trail is encouraged, so our ranger guide had us dismount and traipse through the surrounding pineland and hardwood hammock areas.

As we headed back to our bikes, I must have sensed something amiss, because I glanced down in mid-step to see a small, coiled snake right in front of me. My shriek of surprise brought the ranger over, and he confirmed what I already knew by sight and sound: it was a baby diamondback rattler. What a cute little thing it was, shaking its two little rattler nubs with all its might, like a kid trying to show off how big and strong he was. Everyone came over to look, but the ranger said, "Where there's a baby, there's usually a mama nearby," so we decided we'd best be moving along.

On this visit we discovered an indigenous vine that looks a lot like Silly String. The thin, fluorescent orange filament stealthily creeping through the Everglades is deceptively strong, choking other vegetation and tripping hikers who mistakenly suppose they can plow right through it. Its name? Love vine.

Love exemplified as a snare, a trap, and as suffocating? Not a very pretty picture, is it? Yet that's the way some people see God—as a killjoy who doesn't want them to enjoy life, a tyrant ready to gleefully zap them whenever they step out of line.

I read an article that summed up the main message of parenting this way: have fun but don't die. That just about says it all, doesn't it? From the moment we first hold our children, our primary concerns are keeping them happy and safe. We buy them car seats and feed them nutritious food. Later we admonish them to pay attention when crossing the street and not to talk to strangers, fret about their schooling, and warn them of the dangers of drugs and alcohol. All while trying to make life exciting!

Even when they leave home, we keep at it. Several years ago, I ended a phone call to my mother by telling her I was going out for a bike ride. "Be careful," she said.

"Mom, I'm forty-four years old!" I replied, exasperated.

Mom has the last laugh, as usual. I now find myself doing the same thing to *my* daughter, reminding her to drive carefully, be aware of her surroundings when she's out late, etc. "And have fun!" I add.

Fortunately, Mimi (usually) tolerates this with good humor, and by now she (usually) realizes that I don't say stuff like that because I think she's incapable of looking out for herself. I just can't help myself: I'm her mother! Her welfare will always be my top priority.

I think that's the portrait Scripture paints of God, our Heavenly Father. His cautions, restraints, and admonitions aren't to make our lives miserable or undermine our confidence. He desires us to have an abundant life filled with joy and pleasure, but he also wants to protect us from that which would kill us spiritually, from the world's pythons that would distract us from what's important, from poisonous situations, and the sin that so easily entangles, as Hebrews 12:1 puts it.

As the saying goes, moms have eyes in the back of their heads. Maybe so, but even the best parents can't protect their kids from everything. What I know for sure is that we can't escape God's gaze—and that's a good thing. Because his eyes "range throughout the earth to strengthen those whose hearts are fully committed to him" (2 Chronicles 16:9).

That kind of love will *never* trip us up.

See for Yourself

Everglades National Park: *www.nps.gov/ever*

This wild and wonderful place is directly west of urban Miami-Dade County. At the Ernest F. Coe Visitor Center, sign up for free or low-cost ranger talks, hikes, bike rides, and canoe and kayak trips. Most are offered only in high season, December through April.

The park's main road meanders for thirty-eight miles, and has several short, level hiking trails off it. In the Royal Palm area, the Anhinga Trail is the place to spot the bird it's named after, as well as alligators and turtles. The Gumbo-Limbo Trail is a shady walk through trees of the same name.

Further along is the Pahayokee Overlook, a less than quarter-mile boardwalk that winds through a bald cypress forest and leads to an observation tower offering a panoramic view of the "River of Grass."

Everglades is on the migratory bird route, and many winter over in the park, so stop at Mrazek Pond to spy egrets, roseate spoonbills, and herons, among many other feathered species.

At the end of the road is the Flamingo Visitor Center, where the park's fresh water mingles with salt water from Florida Bay. This is the best spot to find both alligators and crocodiles; Everglades is the only place in the world where they coexist. A tutorial in the Visitor Center will enable you to tell them apart.

If you have time, head to the Shark Valley area on the park's northern border. A fifteen-mile loop path cutting through the freshwater slough (pronounced "slew") allows walkers and bicyclists to get *very* close to gators snoozing in the sun during the winter. A narrated tram tour is available for a fee for those who prefer a little more distance. Another observation tower is at trail's end. Forty-five miles west of there is the Gulf Coast Visitor Center in Everglades City where you can pay for a boat ride through the Ten Thousand Islands and watch dolphins frolic.

My Fellow Churchgoers
Biscayne National Park

The body is a unit, though it is made up of many parts; and though all its parts are many, they form one body. So it is with Christ...In fact God has arranged the parts in the body, every one of them, just as he wanted them to be...so that there should be no division in the body, but that its parts should have equal concern for each other.

1 Corinthians 12:14, 18, 25

Water and mangrove trees are two prominent natural elements in southeastern Florida's Biscayne National Park. About 95 percent of the park is water, with one of the most extensive coral reef tracts in the world, while the mangrove forest that hugs the shoreline is the largest such undeveloped stretch on the East Coast.

As late as the 1960s, mangroves were considered almost worthless. Developers ruthlessly cleared the trees to make way for harbors and houses, their wood used to create charcoal.

Now mangroves are appreciated just as and where they are. Without these sturdy guardians, hurricanes would be even more destructive as they moved inland. Their tangled and weird-looking root system prevents erosion, and filters out silt and pollutants so Biscayne Bay remains sparkling clear. The roots also trap the trees' leaves, which helps stabilize the shore and feed the tiny animals that find shelter there, which in turn become nourishment for other marine life and birds. Mangroves aren't nuisances at all, but necessary and vital links in the ecosystem and food chain.

I sometimes look at people the same way we used to look at mangroves. I fume or shake my head over their lazy ways, their personality rubs me the wrong way, they're odd and disagreeable… well, you get the picture. Anyway, I secretly—and occasionally even out loud—wish *those other people* would pull their own weight, clean up their dysfunctional lives, or just go bother somebody else.

I sure wish life could always be as delightful as the morning I spent on gorgeous Biscayne Bay. Our boat glided past the mangroves as dolphins capered and brown pelicans swooped down for their next meal. The sun shone on the rippling water, and I fantasized what it would be like to spend every weekend lolling on Boca Chita Key. Unfortunately, the crowded harbor and accompanying diesel engine fumes, not to mention too many others with the same idea, spoiled my idyllic dream.

So often I'm guilty of appreciating the natural beauty of the world God made while disparaging his greatest work, the people he made in his own image. How easily I dismiss those who are much more important in his sight than even the most awesome national park!

Yet God sees and loves us just as we are. Like Biscayne's mangroves are to the ecosystem, each of us is a necessary and vital link in God's kingdom. He knits together a ragtag bunch of messy humans for his purposes, and then actually expects us to put up with each other—even the ones we feel serve no purpose than to make life difficult. On such an outrageous premise is the church established: by caring for the "least of these"—and that may include us at times—we serve Christ and proclaim his glory.

Lord, help me value the strange mangroves in my life...especially when I'm one of them.

See for Yourself

Biscayne National Park: *www.nps.gov/bisc.gov*

This is the place to indulge your love of water sports and bird and marine life watching. The Maritime Heritage Trail, the only underwater archaeological trail in the National Park Service, spans a century of maritime history and takes you past six shipwrecks. On land, ranger-led walks go to the best spots for wildlife viewing.

The Dante Fascell Visitor Center, named after the congressman instrumental in creating the park, has a museum detailing the park's four primary ecosystems and a gallery featuring works by local artists inspired by the park. There's a nice view of Biscayne Bay from the rocking chairs on the porch.

Boca Chita Key has a lighthouse, picnic tables and grills, and restrooms, but not fresh water. Campsites and overnight docking here and on the larger island of Elliot Key are available for a fee. Bring mosquito repellent and plan to pack out your trash.

The park holds a no-cost Family Fun Fest the second Sunday afternoon of each month from December through April. Forget the car, and instead hop on the free trolley that runs from the nearby city of Homestead, November through April.

For a memorable winter vacation, do what my husband and I did: set aside a week to take in all three of southern Florida's national parks. Fly into Miami or Fort Lauderdale. Spend at least one day at Biscayne, two to three days in Everglades, then travel to Key West. Reserve a boat tour from there to Dry Tortugas in advance for the following day. Check out the sights in Key West, drive back to the airport, and head home. It's great to swim in the Gulf of Mexico in January!

Justice Now—And Later
War Relocation Centers

These are the things you are to do: Speak the truth to each other, and render true and sound judgment in your courts.

Zechariah 8:16

We tend to think of our national parks in terms of gorgeous scenery and wide-open spaces filled with rarely seen wildlife. Of course, many do fit that description.

We go to them for rest, relaxation, and renewal, to get away from our overcrowded, overscheduled, busy lives. A good idea, generally.

Yet our national park system ultimately is about more than those things. It not only showcases our glorious land, but our history as well. We celebrate our freedom at the Statue of Liberty and the Liberty Bell. We applaud our fighting spirit and honor heroes at battlefields such as Bunker Hill and Gettysburg.

Sometimes, though, our past is not so splendid. The struggle for civil rights, told at places like Little Rock Central High School and Brown

v. Board of Education National Historic Sites, reminds us of times when our country wasn't at its best.

Recently I've been reading about another National Historic Site, one I never knew existed, a location that explores another period of great shame and injustice in our nation. Ironically, it came into existence at a time when we pulled together as never before—except, of course, for those unfortunate enough to be the scapegoats.

In February 1942, President Franklin D. Roosevelt issued Executive Order 9066, ordering the round up and detainment of men, women, and children residing in the United States but deemed possible enemies. The vast majority were resident Japanese aliens and Japanese American citizens on the West Coast, adding up to almost 120,000 people. A much lesser number of German and Italian Americans across the country also were detained. Manzanar, now a National Historic Site, became one of ten war relocation centers where most of those of Japanese ancestry spent the duration of World War II.

While some of the detainees weren't citizens, two-thirds of them were. Yet all of them had to leave their homes, businesses, and schools to live behind barbed wire in military-style camps. Our government exchanged some (both legal aliens and citizens) for American prisoners of war, and simply deported others to their ancestral, war-ravaged countries.

I know it was wartime, and the United States was still reeling from the attack on Pearl Harbor. Fear was rampant. Would there be another invasion? Were our enemies infiltrating the country and working against us? Apprehension filtered down even to the little Illinois town where my grandparents lived—someone smashed their home's picture window because of their German surname.

President Roosevelt had come into office in 1933 in the middle of the Depression, and in his inaugural address, he reassured the nation that "the only thing we have to fear is fear itself." He used that same philosophy to quell these new anxieties, and one of the ways he did that was to round up those who looked like our enemies.

But these internees never experienced one of our country's most cherished principles, stated in Article One of the Constitution, the right not to be detained without a trial.

Eventually, the War Department realized there was a large workforce in the camps that could possibly be helping with the war effort. The government allowed those who gave the "correct" answers on a "loyalty test" to work off-premises to replace farmers called to service. Select students were granted leave to attend college. In perhaps the biggest irony of all, the War Department drafted eligible internees into a special combat troop to fight for the country that held their relatives captive. That group went on to become, for its size and length of service, the most decorated unit in United States military history.

The Civil Liberties Act of 1988 attempted to right the wrong done four decades earlier. Signed by President Reagan, the bill granted $20,000 each in reparations to the formerly interred Japanese Americans or their heirs. In October 1990, a ceremony was held to present the first checks and a formal apology signed by President George H. W. Bush:

> A monetary sum and words alone cannot restore lost years or erase painful memories; neither can they fully convey our Nation's

resolve to rectify injustice and to uphold the rights of individuals. We can never fully right the wrongs of the past. But we can take a clear stand for justice and recognize that serious injustices were done to Japanese Americans during World War II.

In enacting a law calling for restitution and offering a sincere apology, your fellow Americans have in a very real sense, renewed their traditional commitment to the ideals of freedom, equality, and justice. You and your family have our best wishes for the future.

As the president noted, I'm sure even an apology and financial compensation didn't fully right the wrongs done to the survivors or their descendants. Can anything tangible truly make up for inner pain?

Not likely. The administration of justice here on earth will always be imperfect and inadequate, because we ourselves are unjust. This is why we need a personal Justifier, One who covers all the wrongs we've done and the wrongs done to us. Then we can forgive ourselves and others, empowered to "act justly and to love mercy and to walk humbly with God" (Micah 6:8), looking forward to the time when justice will "roll on like a river [and] righteousness like a never-failing stream" (Amos 5:24).

That flood of final, absolute, and perfect judgment will bring "joy to the righteous but terror to evildoers" (Proverbs 21:15), and finally, all the world's injustices will be righted for all time.

That day can't come soon enough.

See It for Yourself

The United States had ten war relocation centers in all, but only a few are in the National Park Service:

- **Manzanar,** located about three-and-a-half hours north of Los Angeles at the foot of the Sierra Nevadas, is the most accessible. Take an auto tour and see reconstructed barracks, a mess hall, and the camp cemetery. You can even pick apples from the remaining trees in the orchard. At the Visitor Center, extensive exhibits detail the detainees' experiences. (*www.nps.gov/manz*)

- **Tule Lake** is in northern California, just south of the Oregon border, and is part of the WWII Valor in the Pacific National Monument. It was the largest Japanese American camp, housing nearly nineteen thousand, including a young George Takei, best known for his role in the original *Star Trek* television series. The Visitor Center, inside the Tulelake-Butte Valley Fairgrounds office, is staffed only between Memorial Day and Labor Day, and ranger tours are offered only on Saturdays. The rest of the year you can pick up brochures and see exhibits at the fairgrounds museum when it's open. (*www.nps.gov/tule*)

- **Minidoka Relocation Center,** a 33,000-acre site, was the seventh largest city in Idaho during its operation. Today a 1.6-mile walking trail dotted with interpretative signs about the camp's history is open all year. (*www.nps.gov/miin*)

- **The Aleutian World War II National Historic Area,** eight hundred miles west of Anchorage, Alaska, tells the story of the only land invasion of Japanese forces in the United States and another mass internment of American civilians. Displaced Unangan (Aleut) people endured extreme hardship while crowded into "duration villages." The site is accessible only by air or ferry. (*www.nps.gov/aleu*)

All Are Welcome
Charles Young Buffalo Soldiers National Monument

I now realize how true it is that God does not show favoritism, but accepts men from every nation who fear him and do what is right.

Acts 10:34

February is Black History Month, a perfect opportunity to recognize one of the newest National Park Service units, the Charles Young Buffalo Soldiers National Monument, established by presidential proclamation in 2013. Black Buffalo Soldiers, like their white counterparts in western United States Army regiments, fought in the Indian Wars and were among the first national park rangers. The Plains Indians gave these cavalry troops their nickname because they thought their hair resembled the dark, curly cushion between a buffalo's horns.

Charles Young was one of those soldiers. Young was born in Kentucky to enslaved parents; his father escaped and served with the Union at the end of the Civil War. His family relocated to Ohio where, after graduating with honors from high school, he taught at an African

American elementary school. His father urged him to take the entrance examination to the United States Military Academy at West Point, and his high score enabled him to enroll in 1884. He became the ninth black to attend West Point and only the third to earn a commission, despite enduring racial insults and social isolation.

Second Lieutenant Young served with the Ninth Cavalry in the West, attaining the rank of captain and fighting with distinction in the Spanish American War. He also taught military science and tactics at Wilberforce University in Ohio.

His stint in the national parks began in 1903. The United States Army had served as administrators of Yosemite and Sequoia National Parks since 1891, wintering at the Presidio in San Francisco and serving in the Sierras during the summer. Captain Young and his company of Buffalo Soldiers were sent into Sequoia in 1903, not only to protect the area but also to better it. Their work building roads and improving the infrastructure allowed the public access to the park for the first time. The captain became the Acting Superintendent of the park that year.

Young went on to a long and distinguished military career, serving in Haiti, the Dominican Republic, Liberia, and Mexico. He was promoted to major, then lieutenant colonel, and finally colonel, before his medical retirement. During World War I, he helped muster and train black recruits. Young died in Nigeria in 1922. When his body was returned to the United States to be buried in Arlington National Cemetery, he received a hero's welcome.

If you've viewed any of the Ken Burns series on the national parks shown on PBS, you may have seen Shelton Johnson, a ranger at Yosemite who also portrays a Buffalo Solider in a one-person show. As a black man, he's in the unique position of being both part of the Park Service and a minority, and he's very aware of the scarcity of people who look like him in the parks, despite stories like Charles Young's. He told the *New York Times* he's more likely to meet someone from Finland or Israel in the parks than someone from Harlem.

My husband and I have noticed the same thing during our many park trips. While Europeans are a common sight, blacks—from here or elsewhere—are not.

Statistics support these observations. According to a 2011 report on racial and ethnic diversity done by the National Park Service, only 22 percent of park visitors are minorities, even though they make up 37 percent of the United States population. "African Americans were the most 'under-represented' visitor group," the report concluded, with Hispanic Americans coming in second.

Fortunately, the Park Service, is looking to remedy the problem, which the director told the *Times* is "a disconnect that needs addressing."

Some of the steps the Park Service is taking to be more welcoming are incorporating stories like that of the Buffalo Soldiers into park tours and brochures, planning partnerships with high schools that arrange park jobs for students, holding more naturalization ceremonies for new citizens in the parks, and recruiting employees at historically black colleges and universities. Having a black family in the White House who has visited national parks has set a powerful example.

The early church had something of a similar disconnect. The book of Acts spans thirty years of transition following Jesus's ascension, as the gospel message moved from mainly a Jewish audience to include

Gentiles as well. Chapters ten, eleven, and fifteen detail the struggle of these two different groups of believers coming to terms with their diverse habits and ways. The church's continued existence depended upon hearing each other's concerns, finding areas of agreement, and hammering out concessions so that everyone, no matter what their heritage or background, would feel welcome in this new religion called Christianity.

Episcopal Bishop James A. Pike stated, in the May 16, 1960 issue of *U.S. News & World Report*, "The 11 o'clock hour on Sunday is the most segregated hour in American life," a phrase later echoed by Dr. Martin Luther King, Jr. Things haven't changed much since then.

Would that we, the church today, follow the example of those first Christians! After all, heaven will be populated with people from every tribe, language, and nation, each one purchased for God with the blood of Jesus. Let's get the party started early!

See for Yourself

Charles Young Buffalo Soldiers National Monument: *www.nps.gov/chyo*

As of this writing, the park in Wilberforce, Ohio, is still being developed, and is open to the public only on select days throughout the year. Check the website's calendar for scheduled events, or go to its social media pages on Facebook, Twitter, Flickr, and Instagram.

Martin Luther King, Jr. Day in January is another fee-free date in the national parks.

To God Be the Glory!

Then the angel showed me the river of the water of life, as clear as crystal, flowing from the throne of God and of the Lamb down the middle of the great street of the city. On each side of the river stood the tree of life, bearing twelve crops of fruit, yielding its fruit each month. And the leaves of the tree are for the healing of the nations.

Revelation 22:1-2

Several years ago, my extended family and I took a trip to the Grand Canyon.

As we flew over northern Arizona, the pilot directed our attention to this huge crack in the earth, and I could almost feel the plane tilt as we all rushed to peer out the right side windows. It's an amazing sight even from thirty thousand feet up.

A few days later, as soon as we pulled up to the canyon's North Rim in our rental cars, we jumped out and ran to the edge—which fortunately is protected by a rock wall, lest dumbstruck tourists like us fall over the cliff in our captivated stupor. I can attest that all seven of our mouths hung open in wonder. Seeing the Grand Canyon up close is even more awesome than observing it from the air.

Over the next few days, we took every opportunity to drink it in. We didn't get to the bottom—the Colorado River, which flows between the two rims, was high and too dangerous to navigate that week. We weren't adventurous enough as a group to hike down and back up again. But we did walk the North Rim trails, rode mules part way down a steep, twisting path that definitely is not for the faint of heart, and ate dinner watching the sun set over the multi-hued strata. Many times we just sat in rocking chairs and stared.

You might have noticed that I haven't described much of the canyon itself. That's because my inadequate words would never be able to properly convey the magnificence, grandeur, and sheer scope of this incredible natural phenomenon. I think that's the point the apostle Paul was trying to make when he wrote in Romans 11:33, "Oh, the depth of the riches of the wisdom and knowledge of God! How unsearchable his judgments, and his paths beyond tracing out!" Words essentially failed him as he tried to articulate how great, how wonderful, how wise the Lord is, and how we'll never entirely plumb the depths of his being.

I haven't learned all the life lessons I've covered here, in case you were wondering. Just because I have my name on a book doesn't mean I have it all figured out, any more than you would. I struggle with many of the things I've written about, still don't get why God sends the rain and the sun on the just and the unjust, or why he chose me for salvation by paying for my sins through the death of his Son Jesus Christ. Or why he's given me the opportunity to travel to so many of these great parks. Like the Grand Canyon, it's way too much for me to take in.

But oh, it's good to know I don't have to—because he has it all covered.

I certainly hope I've piqued your interest in the remarkable treasures that are our national parks. Even more, I pray I've whetted your appetite for the greatest treasure of all—knowing God, and growing deeper in him. He calls all of us to "take hold of the life that is truly life" (1 Timothy 6:19), not only here on earth but in eternity, where there's a crystal clear river and one amazing tree in a park that's really out of this world.

References

SPRING

Badé, William Frederic. 1924. *The Life and Letters of John Muir Vol. 1.* Boston and New York: Houghton Mifflin Company, 209. https://archive.org/stream/lifeandlettersof007082mbp#page/n227/mode/2up

Chesterton, Gilbert K. 1912. *What's Wrong with the World.* New York: Dodd, Mead and Company, 48.

McCullough, David. 1968. *The Johnstown Flood.* New York: Simon & Schuster.

McLean, Allison. 2011. October Anniversaries: Momentous or Merely Memorable. *Smithsonian,* October. http://www.smithsonianmag.com/history/october-anniversaries-4-72394275/?no-ist

N. J. Museum Finds Recording of 19th Century German Chancellor. Associated Press, February 4, 2012. http://www.nj.com/news/index.ssf/2012/02/nj_museum_finds_recording_of_1.html

Shugart, Sharon, 2004. *The Hot Springs of Arkansas Through the Years: A Chronology of Events—Excerpts.* Department of the Interior, National Park Service. http://www.nps.gov/hosp/learn/historyculture/index.htm

Summers, Robert K. 2009. *Dr. Samuel A. Mudd at Fort Jefferson 4th Edition.* Robert K. Summers, 1. http://tinyurl.com/pvnu4b9

SUMMER

Fitch, David E, 2011. *The End of Evangelism? Discerning a New Faithfulness for Mission: Toward an Evangelical Political Theology.* Eugene, Oregon: Cascade Books, 82. http://tinyurl.com/jnke5z2

Franke, Mary Ann. 2000. Yellowstone in the Afterglow: Lessons from the Fires. Yellowstone Center for Resources. Yellowstone National Park. Mammoth Hot Springs, Wyoming. http://www.nps.gov/yell/planyourvisit/upload/full-2.pdf

Hoffman, Thomas J. Sandy Hook's Lifesavers. Sandy Hook. Gateway National Recreation Area. National Park Service. United States Department of the Interior.
http://www.nps.gov/gate/learn/historyculture/upload/history_uslss.pdf

Johnson, Robert Underwood. 1916. "John Muir as I Knew Him." In *Sierra Club Bulletin, Vol. 10, No. 1,* edited by William Frederic Badé. http://vault.sierraclub.org/john_muir_exhibit/life/johnson_tribute_scb_1916.aspx

Kriplen, Nancy. 2009. The Cumberland Gap, the Notch America Squeezed Through. *New York Times*, September 11. http://www.nytimes.com/2009/09/13/travel/13journeys.html?_r=0

Luckett, William W. 1964. Cumberland Gap National Historical Park. The Tennessee Historical Society, Vol. XXIII, No. 4, December. Reprinted 1993. Tennessee Historical Quarterly. http://www.nps.gov/parkhistory/online_books/cuga/luckett/index.htm

National Park Service. Golden Gate National Recreation Area. Parks for the People – Marin County Story panel. http://www.nps.gov/goga/learn/historyculture/parks-for-the-people-marin-county-story-panel.htm

Noble, Dr. Dennis L. A Legacy: The United States Life-Saving Service. United States Life-Saving Service Heritage Association. http://n.b5z.net/i/u/10059514/f/articles/AHistoryoftheUSLSS-DenisNoble.pdf

Noble, Dennis L, 1994. *That Others Might Live: The United States Life-Saving Service, 1878-1915*. Annapolis, Maryland: Naval Institute Press.

Shook, Jeff. 2009. Introduction to the USLSS. United States Life-Saving Service Heritage Association. http://uslife-savingservice.org/about-us/introduction-to-the-uslss/

The Yellowstone Fires of 1988. Yellowstone National Park. National Park Service. United States Department of the Interior. http://www.nps.gov/yell/learn/nature/upload/firesupplement.pdf

Zezima, Katie. 2009. Acadia Park Cracks Down on Rock Thieves. *New York Times*, July 7. http://www.nytimes.com/2009/07/08/us/08rock.html

FALL

Library of Congress. 1995. Gettysburg Address Exhibition Home, January 12-19. https://www.loc.gov/exhibits/gettysburg-address/

Twain, Mark. Introduction to *Mark Twain's Letters from Hawaii*. Ed A. Grove Day. Honolulu: University of Hawaii Press, 1975, xii. http://tinyurl.com/gujljj9

Twain, Mark (Samuel L. Clemens), 1904. *Roughing It in Two Volumes Vol. II*. New York and London: Harper & Brothers Publishers, 315-6. http://tinyurl.com/o5bdwuz

WINTER

Haught, James A. 1996. *2000 Years of Disbelief: Famous People with the Courage to Doubt*. Amherst, New York: Prometheus Books, 315. http://tinyurl.com/qjkvm96

McLellan, Dennis. 2010. Kermit A. Tayler dies at 96; officer didn't act on radar warning about Pearl Harbor raid. *Los Angeles Times*, February 24. http://articles.latimes.com/2010/feb/24/local/la-me-kermit-tyler25-2010feb25

Martin, Joseph Plumb. 2006. *Memoir of a Revolutionary Soldier: The Narrative of Joseph Plumb Martin.* Mineola, New York: Dover Publications, Inc., 102-3.

Miller, Patricia. The Origination of the Luminary, Luminaria, Farolitas or Farolitos. https://flicluminaries.com/content/14-luminary-history

National Park Service. United States Department of the Interior. Natural Resource Stewardship and Science. National Park Service Comprehensive Survey of the American Public 2008-2009. Racial and Ethnic Diversity of National Park System Visitors and Non-Visitors. https://www.nature.nps.gov/socialscience/docs/CompSurve y2008_2009RaceEthnicity.pdf

Navarro, Mireya. 2010. National Parks Reach Out to Blacks Who Aren't Visiting. *New York Times,* November 2. http://www.nytimes. com/2010/11/03/science/earth/03parks.html?_r=0

Unrau, Harlan D. 1996. *The Evacuation and Relocation of Persons of Japanese Ancestry During World War II: A Historical Study of the Manzanar War Relocation Center.* Historic Resource Study/Special History Study. Volumes One and Two. United States Department of the Interior, National Park Service, Epilogue. http://www.nps.gov/ parkhistory/online_books/manz/hrse.htm

Weigley, Russell Frank. 1983. Morristown: A History and Guide, Morristown National Historical Park, New Jersey. Washington, D.C.: Division of Publications, National Park Service, United States Department of the Interior, "About This Book."

About the Author

Penny Musco is a freelance writer and performer with a B.A. in Speech and Dramatic Art from the University of Iowa. Her publishing credits include *Family Circle, More, Costco Connection, Focus on the Family, Mature Living, Evangel, Plain Truth, Power for Living, The War Cry, Today's Christian Woman, Guideposts,* and more.

As the first Artist in Residence at Homestead National Monument in Nebraska, Penny wrote and performed a one-woman show, *Steal Away: The Story of a Homesteader and an Exoduster.* She continues to present the program for community groups and at libraries and senior living residences. Visit the website (*www.steal-away.com*) for more information about this program.

Penny lives in Florida with her husband, a theatre professional. They have an adult daughter. Visit her website to learn more, and to find her blog about the national parks at *www.pennymusco.com*

CPSIA information can be obtained
at www.ICGtesting.com
Printed in the USA
LVOW04s0347060716

495280LV00017B/167/P